WITHDRAWN

FREE MONEY

from Colleges and Universities

OTHER BOOKS BY LAURIE BLUM

Childcare/Education

FREE MONEY FOR DAY CARE

FREE MONEY FOR PRIVATE SCHOOLS

FREE MONEY FOR FOREIGN STUDY

FREE MONEY FOR GRADUATE SCHOOL

FREE MONEY FOR CHILDREN'S MEDICAL EXPENSES

FREE MONEY FOR CHILDHOOD BEHAVIORAL AND GENETIC DISORDERS

Healthcare

FREE MONEY FOR HEART DISEASE AND CANCER CARE

FREE MONEY FOR DISEASES OF AGING

FREE MONEY FOR INFERTILITY TREATMENTS

FREE MONEY FOR MENTAL/EMOTIONAL DISORDERS

The Arts

FREE MONEY FOR PEOPLE IN THE ARTS

Business

FREE MONEY FOR SMALL BUSINESS & ENTREPRENEURS

HOW TO INVEST IN REAL ESTATE USING FREE MONEY

Other

FREE DOLLARS FROM THE FEDERAL GOVERNMENT

THE COMPLETE GUIDE TO GETTING A GRANT

Laurie Blum

FREE MONEY

from Colleges and Universities

HENRY HOLT AND COMPANY

NEW YORK

Henry Holt and Company, Inc.
Publishers since 1866
115 West 18th Street
New York, New York 10011

Henry Holt® is a registered trademark
of Henry Holt and Company, Inc.

Library of Congress Cataloging-in-Publication Data
Blum, Laurie.
Free money from colleges and universities / Laurie Blum. —
1st. ed.
p. cm. — (Free money series)
Includes bibliographical references and index.
1. Scholarships—United States—Directories. 2. Student
aid—United States—Directories. I. Title. II. Series:
Blum, Laurie. Free money series.
LB2337.2.B597 1993   92–44655
378.3'025'73—dc20   CIP

ISBN 0-8050-2657-6
ISBN 0-0850-2658-4 (An Owl Book: pbk.)

First Edition—1993

Printed in the United States of America
All first editions are printed on acid–free paper. ∞

10 9 8 7 6 5 4 3 2 1

10 9 8 7 6 5 4 3 2 1 (pbk)

· · · · · · · · · · · · · · · · · · · ·

With much thanks to Jung Cho, Cybèle Fisher, Janet Mannheimer, Jonathan Struthers, Ken Rose, Paula Kakalecik and Ken Wright

Contents

. . . .

Introduction

Almost every college and university offers scholarships to study at their institution in a wide variety of disciplines. Surprisingly, many students have no idea that these scholarships exist, nor where or how to navigate through the bureaucratic maze of institutional departments or family foundations.

Do you just walk up, hold out your hand, and expect someone to put money in it? Of course not. It takes time, effort, and thought on your part. You're going to have to fill out applications. You may meet with frustration or rejection somewhere down the road. The odds, however, are in your favor that you will qualify for some sort of financial aid.

The hardest part has always been finding these sources of money, which is why I wrote this book. This book provides you, the reader, with the actual sources of monies available.

The listings are organized alphabetically by state with the colleges and universities listed alphabetically within each state. The information is also cross-referenced by subject.

I have included wherever possible the total amount of money that is awarded to students, the number of scholarships or grants given, the average size of an award, and the range of monies given. Do not be dissuaded from applying if the average award is only $200 (the same material you put together for one application can be used for most, if not all, of the other applications; you will hopefully apply for a number of scholarships and grants). You might get more, you might get less. But remember, this is free money!

HOW TO APPLY

Applying for grants and scholarships is a lot like applying for school: it takes work, thought and organization. But at this stage in your life, you know what you have to do. You've done this before.

First comes the sorting out process. Go through this book and mark off all the listings that could give you money. Pay close attention to the restrictions and eliminate the least likely foundations. Although none of the foundations in this book require an application fee, the effort you'll have to put in will probably limit you to no more than eight applications (if you are ambitious and want to apply to more than eight foundations, bravo, go right ahead). Write or call the most likely foundations to get a copy of their guidelines. (In cases where the contact's name is not listed, begin your letter: To Whom It May Concern). If you call, just request the guidelines; don't interrogate the poor person who answers the phone.

Grant applications, like college applications, take time to fill out. Often you will be required to write one or more essays. Be neat! You may very well prepare a top-notch proposal, but it won't look good if it's done in a sloppy manner. Proposals should always be typed, double-spaced, and be sure to make a copy of the proposal. I've learned the hard way that there is nothing worse than having to reconstruct it because you didn't keep a copy. Many applications will require any previous college transcripts. Often the tax returns of both the applicant (if you had filed a return the previous year) and your parents are needed. Sometimes an interview is required (you probably had some interviews when you were looking at colleges, right?) You may be asked to include personal references (be sure to notify the people you are planning to use as references; there is nothing worse than having a foundation contact your reference, who has no idea what it is about). Remember, you have to sell yourself and convince the grantors to give money to you and not to someone else.

OTHER SOURCES OF MONEY

Many millions of dollars in athletic scholarships go unclaimed each year simply because no one applied for them, or because the athletic departments couldn't find enough qualified applicants.

Before you reject this category because you are not a 250-pound left tackle or do not have the backhand of Chris Evert, consider the following:

Until the late 1970's it was all too common for colleges to have multimillion dollar training facilities for the football and basketball teams, while the women's volleyball team practiced on a muddy lot with a clothesline stretched between two poles. A law that took effect in 1978 decreed that schools must provide male and female athletes with "equal benefits and opportunities." That means separate but equal practice facilities, equipment, number of games and scholarship money.

In the late 1970's and early 1980's the sports pages were filled with tales of academic abuses committed by outstanding athletes. There are now restrictions on how poorly the star quarterback can do academically before he is asked to leave school. One of the results of these scandals is the limit imposed by a school on how many scholarships can be awarded in the "major" sports (football, basketball, track and field, softball), with requirements that money be distributed among women athletes in these sports, as well as in archery, badminton, bowling, crew, Frisbee (yes, there is a scholarship currently available at the State University of New York at Purchase, albeit just one), handball, and synchronized swimming (this is a sport available only to women athletes; did Esther Williams stereotype us all?)

Schools are not restricted in how they spend their recruiting time and effort, only their scholarship money. Consequently, they will often devote a considerable amount of time and effort seeking out the best archery, bowling or lacrosse athletes. If someone happens to turn up and ask for scholarship money, fine. If not, the money goes back into the general fund. No big deal. "Wide World of Sports" hasn't paid a dime for the rights to collegiate riflery! So be sure not to neglect some of your less obvious skills; one of them might help pay for your college education.

Finally, be sure to request information from your high school guidance counselor and the financial aid office at each school you have applied to. They can explain what scholarships or other forms of aid the university offers.

Paying for college isn't a one-year, one-shot deal. You must think in terms of this year's costs, next year's costs, and the following year's costs. If tuition charges strain you now, how desperate are you going to be by the time you are a junior?

ONE FINAL NOTE

An asterisk next to a listing indicates that both undergraduate as well as graduate students are eligible for this award.

By the time this book is published, some of the information contained here will have changed. No reference book can be as up to date as the reader or author would like. Names, addresses, dollar amounts, telephone numbers, and other data are always in flux; however, most of the information will not have changed.

— Good luck!

FREE MONEY
from Colleges
and Universities

Free Money from Colleges and Universities

• • • • • • • • • • • • • • • • • •

ALABAMA

Alabama Agricultural and Mechanical University Academic Achievement Scholarships
P.O. Box 908
Normal, AL 35762
(205) 851-5245

Description: Scholarships for undergraduates
Restrictions: Student must have high grades.
$ Given: 165 grants totaling $211,490
Application Information: Formal application is required.
Deadline: April 1
Contact: Mr. James Heyward, Director of Admissions

Alabama State University Presidential Scholarship
915 South Jackson Street
Montgomery, AL 36101-0271
(205) 293-4324

Description: Scholarships for freshmen and juniors
Restrictions: Student must have SAT score of 840 or ACT score of 20 and a 3.5 GPA.
$ Given: 129 grants of $1,626-$4,396; general range: $3,436
Application Information: Submit a handwritten essay detailing career goals.
Deadline: June 1
Contact: Dr. Robert Thompson, Dean of College of Arts and Sciences

Auburn University Phi Eta Sigma Founders Scholarship Awards * Freshman Honor Society
c/o Auburn University
228 JE Foy Union Building
Alabama 36849
(205) 826-5856

Description: Scholarships for undergraduates or first-year graduate students
Restrictions: Student must be a member of Phi Eta Sigma entering first year of graduate, professional or undergraduate studies.
$ Given: 22 grants of up to $1,000 each for undergraduates, 10 grants of up to $2,000 each for first year graduates
Application Information: Write or call for guidelines.
Deadline: March 1
Contact: Faculty Advisor of local chapter

. . . .

Jacksonville
State University
Faculty Scholar Award
Pelham Road
Jacksonville, AL 36265
(205) 782-5006

Description: Scholarships for freshmen
Restrictions: Student must be a resident of Alabama and maintain a 3.25 GPA.
$ Given: 120 grants of $1,200
Application Information: Write for guidelines.
Deadline: April 1
Contact: Larry Smith, Financial Aid Director

Mobile College
Sam & Carrie McDonald
Scholarship Fund
P.O. Drawer 2527
Mobile, AL 36622
APPLICATION ADDRESS:
Financial Aid Office Mobile
College, P.O. Box 13220
Mobile, AL 36613

Description: Scholarships for students of Mobile College
Restrictions: See above.
$ Given: 21 grants totaling $9,025; general range: $150-$550
Application Information: Formal application is required.
Deadline: May 1
Contact: Charles Gambrell, Director of Financial Aid

Springhill College
Lloyd Batre Scholarship
Trust Fund
P.O. Drawer 2527
Mobile, AL 36622
APPLICATION ADDRESS:
Financial Aid Office Springhill
College, 4000 Dauphin Street
Mobile, AL 36622
(205) 460-2140

Description: Scholarships for students attending Springhill College
Restrictions: See above.
$ Given: $8,000 for 4 grants of $2,000 each
Application Information: Formal application is required.
Deadline: None
Contact: Dr. Ben Shearer

• • • • • • • • • • • • • • • • • • •

**University of
South Alabama
Drama Scholarship**
230 Administration Building
Mobile, AL 36688
(205) 460-6101

Description: Scholarships for the study of drama
Restrictions: Scholarship recipients are selected by the faculty of the university.
$ Given: 8 grants of $1,300
Application Information: Contact the university drama department; write for guidelines.
Deadline: N/A
Contact: Drama Department

**University of Alabama
At Birmingham**
University Center
Birmingham, AL 35294
(205) 934-8223

Description: Financial assistance for undergraduates includes: The Francis Depuis Scholarship for Engineering Majors, and The Rime Scholarship for Business Majors.
Restrictions: Residency of Alabama is required from some scholarship recipients.
$ Given: 67 freshman grants totaling $107,000
Application Information: Formal application is required.
Deadline: May 1
Contact: Ms. Janet B. May, Assistant Director of Financial Aid

**University of Alabama
In Huntsville**
Huntsville, AL 35899
(205) 895-6241

Description: Scholarships for undergraduate students includes The Carl T. Jones Scholarships for Engineering, The George W. Ditto Scholarships for Science and Engineering, The Joann Sloan Memorial Scholarships for Nursing, and The Kelly Zettle Scholarships for Music.
Restrictions: Must be native of or resident of Alabama.
$ Given: N/A
Application Information: Formal application is required.
Deadline: April 1
Contact: Mr. Jim Gibson, Director of Financial Aid

• •

University of Alabama Medical School in Birmingham *
Leisa Chambless Endowment
Scholarship Fund
P.O. Box 4540
Montgomery, AL 36195

Description: Scholarships for first-year female medical students at the University of Alabama in Birmingham
Restrictions: Must be a resident of Alabama for at least seven years.
$ Given: 2 grants of $4,677; general range: $577-$4,100
Application Information: Write a letter of 1000 words describing applicant's medical career intentions; include college transcripts, Medical Board scores, and letters of reference.
Deadline: May 1
Contact: N/A

University of Alabama at Birmingham Forensics Scholarship
University Center Box 69
Birmingham, AL 35294
(205) 934-8223

Description: Scholarships for first-year University of Alabama forensics students who win a specific debate tournament
Restrictions: Students must maintain a 3.0 GPA.
$ Given: 8-10 grants of $1,000 each
Application Information: Write for guidelines.
Deadline: N/A
Contact: Dr. Mike Dickman

University of Alabama at Tuscaloosa Computer-Based Honors Scholarship
Box 870162
Tuscaloosa, AL 35487-0162
(205) 348-6756

Description: Scholarships for freshmen
Restrictions: Student must have a ACT score of 31 or a 1300 SAT score
$ Given: 5 grants of $2,000 each
Application Information: Interviews are required.
Deadline: December 20
Contact: Marie Sanders, Scholarship Coordinator

**University of Alabama
at Tuscaloosa
Junior College
Honors Scholarship**
Box 870162
Tuscaloosa, AL 35487-0162
(205) 348-6756

Description: Scholarships for junior college transfer students
Restrictions: Students must have a 3.5 GPA and maintain at least a 3.0 GPA.
$ Given: 5 grants of $1,936 each
Application Information: Write for guidelines.
Deadline: March 7
Contact: Marie Sanders, Program Coordinator

ALASKA

**Alaska Bible College
Freshmen Scholarships**
Glennallen, AK 99588
(907) 822-3201

Description: Scholarships for freshmen
Restrictions: Students must be residents of Alaska
$ Given: 2 grants totaling $3,520
Application Information: Write for guidelines.
Deadline: None
Contact: Mrs. Carolyn King, Financial Aid Officer

Alaska Yukon Pioneers
2725-71 East Fir
Mt. Vernon, WA 98273
(206) 428-1912

Description: Scholarships for students attending University of Alaska, Fairbanks or the University of Alaska, Anchorage
Restrictions: Students must be residents of Alaska.
$ Given: Unspecified number of grants of $2,500
Application Information: Write for guidelines.
Deadline: N/A
Contact: Vera J. Sidars

ALASKA

· · · · · · · · · · · · · · · · · · ·

Sheldon Jackson College
Grotto Foundation Grant
801 Lincoln
Sitka, AK 99835
(907) 747-5241

Description: Scholarships for junior and senior undergraduates
Restrictions: Student must be a resident of Alaska and be studying in the natural resources or aquatic resources program.
$ Given: 11 grants of $1,500-$4,000; general range: $3,000
Application Information: Write for guidelines.
Deadline: March 10
Contact: Dick Goff, Financial Aid Director

University of
Alaska Anchorage
Scholarship Awards
Office of Student Financial Aid
Anchorage, AK 99508
(907) 786-1332

Description: Scholarships for undergraduates, including grants for creative arts, achievement and athletics
Restrictions: See above.
$ Given: 204 grants of various amounts awarded including tuition waivers
Application Information: Write for guidelines.
Deadline: May 15
Contact: Jim Upchurch, Director of Student Financial Aid

University of
Alaska Fairbanks
Scholarship Awards
Office of Financial Aid
Fairbanks, AK 99775
(907) 474-7256

Description: Scholarships for undergraduates for creative arts, athletics and achievement
Restrictions: See above.
$ Given: 350 grants of up to $1,600
Application Information: Formal application is required.
Deadline: May 15
Contact: Don Scheaffer, Director of Financial Aid

• • • • • • • • • • • • • • • • • • • •

ARIZONA

**American Graduate
School of International
Management
Worldwide Assistantship ***
Thunderbird Campus
15249 North 59th Avenue
Glendale, AZ 85306
(602) 978-7130

Description: Graduate scholarships for students interested in international management
Restrictions: See above.
$ Given: 25 grants of $4,535 each
Application Information: Write for guidelines.
Deadline: March 1, October 1
Contact: Catherine King-Todd, Financial Aid Officer

**Arizona State University
Leadership Scholarship**
Tempe, AZ 85287-1602
(602) 965-3355

Description: Scholarships for undergraduates
Restrictions: Students must be residents of Arizona, rank in top 20% of class, and have a 3.0 GPA.
$ Given: 15 grants of $1,300-$1,600
Application Information: Interview is required, references are recommended.
Deadline: January
Contact: University office

**Arizona State University
Library Training Fellowship ***
Tempe, AZ 85287-1602
(602) 965-3355

Description: Graduate fellowships in library science
Restrictions: Applicants must be Native American.
$ Given: 2 grants of $8,000
Application Information: Grants are given by U.S. Department of Education through Arizona State University.
Deadline: N/A
Contact: University Financial Aid Office

Arizona State University PepsiCo. Scholars MBA Fellowships *
College of Business Administration
BAC 600, Arizona State University
Tempe, AZ 85287
(602) 965-5516

Description: Graduate fellowships to first-year students in the MBA program
Restrictions: Students must be studying graduate Management Administration; minority students should especially apply.
$ Given: $3,000 plus tuition first year; graduate assistantships provided second year.
Application Information: Provide test scores and community service record.
Deadline: N/A
Contact: Dean, College of Business Administration

DeVry Institute of Technology Scholarship
2149 West Dunlap
Phoenix, AZ 85021
(602) 870-9201

Description: Scholarships for freshmen majoring in business, electronics or computer systems
Restrictions: See above.
$ Given: 30 grants of $3,648-$7,297 for two years
Application Information: Submit ACT or SAT scores.
Deadline: March 25
Contact: N/A

University of Arizona Baird Scholarship
Tucson, AZ 85721-0007
(602) 621-3237

Description: Scholarships for freshmen
Restrictions: Student must have graduated from a high school in Arizona and maintain a 3.5 GPA.
$ Given: 100 grants of $1,500
Application Information: Write for guidelines.
Deadline: N/A
Contact: J.J. Humphrey, Director/Scholarship Development

. . . .

University of Arizona
College of Education
Graduate Fellowships
in Education *
Office of Student Affairs
University of Arizona
Tucson, AZ 85721

Description: Graduate scholarships for students at University of Arizona with a 3.5 GPA undergraduate in elementary or secondary education.
Restrictions: See above.
$ Given: $10,000 plus tuition
Application Information: Write letter of interest.
Deadline: March 15
Contact: Office of Student Affairs

University of Arizona
John P. Schaefer Honors
Scholarship
Tucson, AZ 85721-0007
(602) 621-3237

Description: Scholarships for freshmen from Arizona high schools who study at the University of Arizona
Restrictions: See above.
$ Given: 100 grants of $1,000 each
Application Information: Write for guidelines.
Deadline: N/A
Contact: J.J. Humphrey, Director/Scholarship Development

V.M. Slipher
Testamentary Trust
c/o Valley Bank Trust Division
P.O. Box 1209
Flagstaff, AZ 86002
APPLICATION ADDRESSES:
Science Departments of
Northern Arizona University,
Arizona State University, and
the University of Arizona.

Description: Scholarships for science students at Northern Arizona University, Arizona State University, and the University of Arizona
Restrictions: Students must be recommended by department heads.
$ Given: $6,440 for 7 grants of $920 each.
Application Information: Write for guidelines.
Deadline: Varies
Contact: The University Scholarship Office at each school

. . . .

ARKANSAS

Arkansas
Technical University
Academic Scholarship
Highway 7
Russellville, AR 72801-2222
(501) 968-0399

Description: Scholarships for freshmen
Restrictions: Students must be residents of Arkansas, have ACT score of 24 and maintain a 3.0 GPA.
$ Given: 150 grants of $1,600; general range: $1,200
Application Information: Write for guidelines.
Deadline: March 15
Contact: Shirley Goines, Director of Student Aid

Harding University
H.Y. Benedict Fellowships
National Council
of Alpha Chi
Harding University *
Box 773
Searcy, AR 72143-5590
(501) 268-3121

Description: Graduate fellowships for members who are nominated in their first year of graduate study in any field.
Restrictions: Must be a member of one of 275 chapters of Alpha Chi and be nominated.
$ Given: N/A
Application Information: Formal application is required.
Deadline: February 22
Contact: Dr. Joseph E. Pryor, Executive Director

Ouachita Baptist University
Publications Scholarship
QBU Box 3774
410 Ouachita Street
Arkadelphia, AR 71923
(501) 246-4531

Description: Scholarships for sophomore, junior and senior undergraduates who are members of the newspaper staff, editors of the yearbook and student photographers.
Restrictions: See above.
$ Given: 3 grants of $4,350 awarded
Application Information: Write for guidelines.
Deadline: N/A
Contact: Dr. Downs, Chairman, Department of Communications

University of Arkansas
Graduate School
U.S. Department
of Education
Graduate and Professional
Program Scholarships *
2801 South University
Little Rock, AR 72204
(501) 569-3327

Description: Graduate scholarships for students at the Unversity of Arkansas with financial need who are majoring in communication disorders
Restrictions: See above.
$ Given: 2 grants of $8,400
Application Information: Write for guidelines.
Deadline: N/A
Contact: University of Arkansas Graduate School

University of Arkansas Art
Graduate Assistantships
University of Arkansas
Fulbright College of Arts
and Sciences *
Art Department
FA 116
Fayetteville, AR 72701
(501) 575-5202

Description: Graduate scholarships and teaching assistantships
Restrictions: Students must have a 2.5 GPA.
$ Given: $2,500 plus tuition first year, $5,000 for second year students.
Application Information: Write for guidelines
Deadline: April 1
Contact: MFA Graduate Coordinator, Art Department

CALIFORNIA

California College of Arts
and Crafts Scholarship *
5212 Broadway
Oakland, CA 94618
(415) 653-8118

Description: Scholarships for both undergraduates and graduates
Restrictions: Students must maintain high grades and demonstrate financial need.
$ Given: 270 grants ranging $1,000-$8,600
Application Information: Write for guidelines.
Deadline: March 1
Contact: Sheri McKenzie, Associate Director, Enrollment

• • • • • • • • • • • • • • •

California State Library Minority Recruitment Scholarship *
The Ramona Building
1001 Sixth Street
Suite 300
Sacramento, CA 95814
(916) 323-4400

Description: Scholarships for minority graduate students in California who are Native American, Asian/Pacific, black or Hispanic and who are interested in pursuing a masters degree in library science
Restrictions: Restricted to three accredited Schools of Library Science in California.
$ Given: 20-40 grants ranging $1,500-$5,000
Application Information: Write for guidelines.
Deadline: May 15
Contact: Rhonda Rios Kravitz

California State University, Fullerton Western Association of Food Chains Scholarship
800 North State
College Boulevard
McCarthy Hall 63
Fullerton, CA 92631
(714) 773-2361

Description: Scholarships for students majoring in business administration/management
Restrictions: Students must show financial need and good grades.
$ Given: 5 grants of $1,000
Application Information: Write for guidelines.
Deadline: March 15
Contact: N/A

Chapman College Academic Performance Scholarship
333 North Glassell Street
Orange, California 92666
(714) 997-6741

Description: Scholarships for freshmen
Restrictions: Student must have a 3.0 GPA and maintain at least a 2.75 GPA.
$ Given: 35 grants of $2,000-$6,600; general range: $4,300
Application Information: Write for guidelines.
Deadline: March 2
Contact: Phyllis Coldiron, Director of Financial Aid

• • • • • • • • • • • • • • • • • • •

**California Western
School of Law
Law Scholarship
Program for Librarians**
350 Cedar Street
San Diego, CA 92101
(619) 239-0391

Description: Scholarships for librarians holding MLS degrees from ALA-accredited schools to study law at California Western School of Law; recipients chosen on the basis of academic achievement, LSAT scores, and personal interview; preference for applicants planning careers in law librarianship
Restrictions: Applicants must have already been accepted by California Western School of Law
$ Given: An unspecified number of full-tuition scholarships are awarded annually
Application Information: Contact Admissions Office for details
Deadline: None
Contact: Admissions Office

**Los Angeles City College
Alpha Mu Gamma National
Scholarships**
855 North Vermont Avenue
Los Angeles, CA 90029
(213) 669-4255

Description: Scholarships for members to study at L.A City College and also Monterey Institute of International Studies
Restrictions: See above.
$ Given: 3 grants of $500 each
Application Information: Write for guidelines.
Deadline: N/A
Contact: Barbara Benjamin, National Executive Secretary

**Samuel Merritt College
Dean's Scholars Program**
370 Hawthorne Avenue
Oakland, CA 94609
(415) 420-6131

Description: Scholarships for freshmen nursing students
Restrictions: Student must have a 3.0-3.4 GPA and maintain at least a 3.0 GPA
$ Given: 19 grants of $2,000-3,000 each
Application Information: Write for guidelines.
Deadline: None
Contact: Mary Robinson, Financial Aid Director

CALIFORNIA

· ·

Sigma Delta Chi
Journalism Scholarships
Bill Farr & Ken Inouye
Scholarships
Los Angeles Chapter
4310 Coronet Drive
Encino, CA 91396

Description: Scholarships for journalism students in the Los Angeles area who are attending four-year colleges in L.A. or Orange Counties
Restrictions: See above.
$ Given: $1,000
Application Information: Write for guidelines
Deadline: December 1
Contact: T.W. McGarry, Scholarship Committee Chair

Stanford University
Fellowship Program *
Stanford Humanities Center
Mariposa House
Stanford, CA 94305-8630
(415) 723-3052

Description: Graduate research fellowships for tenured or untenured Ph.D. candidates who are interested in studying/teaching in the humanities
Restrictions: See above.
$ Given: 6 fellowships which include salaried stipends
Application Information: Write for guidelines.
Deadline: November 15
Contact: Fellowship Program

Stanford University
Center for East Asian
Studies Fellowships *
300 Lasuen Street
Littlefield Center, Room 14
Stanford, CA 94305-5013

Description: Graduate scholarships for students of Stanford University who have interests in linguistics, history, political science or archaeology and who study the cultures of China, Korea or Japan
Restrictions: See above.
$ Given: Grants vary.
Application Information: Write for guidelines.
Deadline: December 31
Contact: Center of East Asian Studies

• • • • • • • • • • • • • • • • • • • •

Stanford University Foreign Language Area Studies Fellowships *
Stanford University Institute of International Studies
300 Lasuen Street, Room 14
Middlefield Center
Stanford, CA 94305-5013
(415) 723-2178

Description: Graduate scholarships for international studies majors studying the following foreign languages: Hausa, Swahili, Arabic, Japanese, Chinese, Korean, Spanish, Portuguese or Russian
Restrictions: See above.
$ Given: $7,000 plus stipend
Application Information: Write for guidelines.
Deadline: January 16
Contact: Marianne Villanueva, Fellowship Coordinator

University of California, Los Angeles Chicano Studies Graduate Fellowships *
405 Hilgard Avenue
180 Haines Hall
Los Angeles, CA 90024-1544

Description: Graduate scholarships for students participating in the Chicano Studies Research Center
Restrictions: Must be a UCLA graduate student in Chicago Research Center
$ Given: $23,000-$28,000
Application Information: Write for guidelines.
Deadline: December 31
Contact: Antonio Serrata, Fellowship Director

University of Southern California All-University Predoctoral Merit Fellowships *
The Graduate School
Los Angeles, CA 90089-4015
(213) 743-5175

Description: Graduate scholarships for students pursuing their PhD degrees at University of Southern California
Restrictions: Graduate students and college seniors
$ Given: $14,000 plus full tuition
Deadline: February 1
Contact: Barbara Solomon, Dean of Graduate Studies

CALIFORNIA

• • • • • • • • • • • • • • • • • • •

University of
Southern California
William M. Keck
Fellowships *
The Graduate School
Los Angeles, CA 90089-4015
(213) 743-5175

Description: Graduate scholarships for minority students pursuing a PhD and career in university teaching and research
Restrictions: Minority student must be American Indian, Alaskan Native (Eskimo or Aleutian), black American, Hispanic or Latino American or Native Pacific Islander.
$ Given: Varies, up to 3 years tuition
Deadline: February 1
Contact: Barbara Solomon, Dean of Graduate Studies

COLORADO

Adams State College
National Scholarship
Financial Aid Office
Alamosa, CO 81102
(719) 589-7306

Description: Scholarships for undergraduates
Restrictions: Students must have ACT scores of 21, cannot be residents of Colorado and must maintain a 2.5 GPA.
$ Given: 200 grants of $1,728 each
Application Information: Write for guidelines.
Deadline: August 15
Contact: Ted Laws, Director of Financial Aid

Colorado College
Barnes Chemistry
Scholarship
14 East Cache La Poudre
Colorado Springs, CO 80903
(719) 389-6431

Description: Scholarships for freshmen chemistry majors
Restrictions: Student must have high grades and plan to be a chemistry major.
$ Given: 21 grants of $13,665 each
Application Information: Write for guidelines.
Deadline: March
Contact: William Champion, Professor of Chemistry

• • • • • • • • • • • • • • • • • • • •

Colorado State University Moorman Company Fund Scholarship
Fort Collins, CO. 80523
(303) 491-1101

Description: Scholarships for students in the College of Agricultural Sciences
Restrictions: Must be interested in agriculture, have financial need and a minimum 3.0 G.P.A.
$ Given: 4 grants of $1,000 each awarded
Application Information: Write for guidelines.
Deadline: February 15
Contact: N/A

Colorado State University Philip A. Connolly Scholarship
College of Forestry and Natural Resources
Fort Collins, CO 80523
(303) 491-1101

Description: Scholarships for students in the College of Forestry and Natural Resources
Restrictions: Student must have financial need, a 3.0 G.P.A. and be in their Junior or Senior year.
$ Given: 5 awards of at least $1,000 each
Application Information: Write for guidelines.
Deadline: February 15
Contact: N/A

Colorado State University Claude W. Wood Scholarship
Fort Collins, CO 80523
(303) 491-1101

Description: Scholarships for freshmen engineering majors
Restrictions: Students must have high grades and a 3.5 GPA
$ Given: 12 grants of $1,500 each
Application Information: Write for guidelines.
Contact: N/A

CONNECTICUT

Central Connecticut State University Honors Scholarship
1615 Stanley Street
New Britain, CT 06050
(203) 827-7305

Description: Scholarships for freshmen and sophomores
Restrictions: See above.
$ Given: 24 grants of $1,865 each
Application Information: Write for guidelines.
Contact: Admissions Office

• • • • • • • • • • • • • • • • • • • •

University of Bridgeport
N. Donald Edwards
Scholarship in Marketing
126 Park Avenue
Wahlstrom Library
Bridgeport, CT 06601
(203) 576-4552

Description: Scholarships for undergraduates
Restrictions: Must be a high school graduate in the top 10%
of the class, and have completed Junior Achievement in
applied economics or a company program.
$ Given: Unspecified number of grants of $1,000 each
Application Information: Write for guidelines.
Deadline: April 1
Contact: Director of Admissions/Junior Achievement Award

University of Connecticut
Alumni Scholarship
c/o Alumni Association
P.O. Box 453
Storrs, CT 06269-3093
(203) 486-2000

Description: Scholarships for undergraduates
Restrictions: Student must show financial requirements.
$ Given: 30 awards of $1,000 each
Application Information: Write for guidelines.
Deadline: Fall
Contact: Alumni Association

Universtity of Hartford
Hartford Art School Artistic
Merit Scholarships
200 Bloomfield Avenue
West Hartford, CT 06117
(203) 243-4827

Description: Scholarships for students in the School of Art
or Media
Restrictions: Student must be in top 10% of class with S.A.T.
scores greater than 1000.
$ Given: Varies.
Application Information: Present written statement of goals
and 20 slides to Admission Committee.
Deadline: February 1
Contact: Wendy Jackson, Admissions Officer

University of New Haven
Echlein Family Scholarship
300 Orange Avenue
West Haven, CT 06516
(203) 932-7315

Description: Scholarships for engineering or business
majors with financial needs
Restrictions: See above.
$ Given: 5 grants of $2,000 each
Application Information: Write for guidelines.
Deadline: N/A
Contact: University Financial Aid Office

• • • • • • • • • • • • • • • • • • • •

University of New Haven
Cheseborough-Ponds
Engineering Scholarship
300 Orange Avenue
West Haven, CT 06516
(203) 932-7315

Description: Scholarships for minority engineering majors
Restrictions: See above.
$ Given: 5 grants of $2,500 each
Application Information: Write for guidelines.
Deadline: N/A
Contact: Office of Financial Aid

Yale University
Yale Center for
British Art-Paul Mellon
Center for Studies
in British Art *
1080 Chapel Street
Box 2120 Yale Station
New Haven, CT 06520
(203) 432-2822

Description: Fellowships for scholars of literature, history or art to research at the Yale Center for British Art
Restictions: See above.
$ Given: Grants for room, board and travel to/from the Center.
Application Information: Write for guidelines.
Deadline: December 31
Contact: The Director, Yale Center for British Art

DELAWARE

American Association
of University Women
Upperclassmen Schools
for Women Residents of
Delaware *
1800 Fairfax Boulevard
Wilmington, DE 19803
(302) 428-0939

Description: Scholarships for junior and senior undergraduates as well as graduate students in Delaware
Restrictions: Female residents of Delaware pursuing an education at Delaware institutions
$ Given: 2 grants up to $1,000 each
Application Information: Write for guidelines.
Deadline: January
Contact: American Association, Delaware branch

Goldey-Beacom College
Scholarship for Academic
Excellence
4701 Limestone Road
Wilmington, DE 19808
(302) 998-8814

Description: Scholarships for undergraduates
Restrictions: Students must have a 3.0 GPA or SAT score of 1050 and work 5 hours/week for the college.
$ Given: 22 grants of $1,500 each
Application Information: Write for guidelines.
Deadline: March 31
Contact: High School Guidance Department

DELAWARE

• •

University of Delaware
Hagley Museum & Library
Fellowship *
Newark, DE 19716
(302) 451-8226

Description: Graduate scholarships for students pursuing a M.A. or PhD and plan careers in museum work, college teaching or research in the history of industrialization
Restrictions: See above.
$ Given: 4-6 fellowships of $9,100-$10,080 each; tuition is fully paid.
Application Information: Personal interviews, GRE scores and recommendations are required.
Deadline: February 1
Contact: Associate Coordinator, Department of History

University of Delaware
Lois F. McNeil Fellowships *
Winterthur Program
Newark, DE 19716

Description: Graduate fellowships for students of art history, literature, folklore, or American studies
Restrictions: College seniors or graduate students may apply.
$ Given: 10 grants of $9,000 plus tuition
Application Information: Formal application required; submit 3-5 page proposal, resume and two letters of recommendation.
Deadline: February 1
Contact: Director, Winterthur Program

DISTRICT OF COLUMBIA

Catholic University
of America
Columbus School of Law
Arnold and Porter
Scholarship *
204 Keane Building
Washington, DC 20064
(202) 319-5143

Description: Scholarships for law students
Restrictions: Student must be a minority second-year law student.
$ Given: 1 grant of $4,000
Application Information: Write for guidelines.
Deadline: April 15
Contact: Marya Dennis, Director of Financial Aid/Law School

Catholic University of America Columbus School of Law Vernon X. Miller Scholarship *
204 Keane Building
Washington DC 20064
(202) 319-5143

Description: Scholarships for law students
Restrictions: Student must have high grades.
$ Given: 7 grants of $1,000-$1,500 each
Application Information: Write for guidelines.
Deadline: June 1
Contact: Marya Dennis, Director of Financial Aid/Law School

Georgetown University Chemistry Department Graduate Research Fellowship *
Department of Chemistry
Box OP
Washington, D.C. 20057
(202) 687-6073

Description: Fellowships for graduate students who must help teach undergraduate courses for one year during their graduate work.
Restrictions: Candidate must have bachelors of science degree in chemistry or equivalent.
$Given: $9000 for 9 months or $10,800 for one year plus tuition waiver valued at no more than $9,800 per year.
Application Information: Write for guidelines.
Deadline: N/A
Contact: Joseph E. Earley, Chairperson at above address.

George Washington University George McCandlish Fellowship in American Literature *
Department of English
Washington, D.C. 20052

Description: Fellowship for graduate student in American Literature (M.A. or Ph.D. program)
Restrictions: Limited to one superior candidate with G.P.A. of 3.25 or above.
$ Given: N/A
Application Information: Write for guidelines.
Deadline: Varies
Contact: Director of Graduate Studies at above address

• •

Howard University
National Competitive
Scholarship
2400 6th Street, NW
Washington, DC 20059
(202) 806-2800

Description: Renewable scholarships for incoming freshmen
Restrictions: Candidates must have exceptional academic records and have a combined SAT score of 1000.
$ Given: 100 grants averaging $8,000 or more
Application Information: Write for guidelines.
Deadline: N/A
Contact: Adrienne Price, Director of the Office of Financial Aid

Paul H. Nitze
School of Advanced
International Studies *
Admissions Office, SAIS
1740 Massachusetts Avenue, NW
Washington, DC 20036

Description: Graduate scholarships for students with a background in international economics and history
Restrictions: Students must have a B.A.
$ Given: Grants vary; cover partial or full tuition at the school.
Application Information: Write for guidelines.
Deadline: February 1
Contact: Admissions Office

Trinity College
Distinguished
Scholar Award
Washington, DC 20017
(202) 269-2201

Description: Scholarships to female undergraduates
Restrictions: Students must have an 1100 SAT score
$ Given: 20 grants of $2,000 each
Application Information: Write essay on the strengths of a woman's college
Deadline: February 15
Contact: N/A

• • • • • • • • • • • • • • • • • • • •

FLORIDA

Baptist Hospital Nursing Education Scholarship
1000 West Moreno Street
Pensacola, FL 32501
(904) 434-4911

Description: Scholarships for nursing students
Restrictions: Students must sign a contract to work at Baptist Hospital upon graduating program; if not, grant money must be returned with 7% interest.
$ Given: 20 grants of $1,500 each
Application Information: Write for guidelines.
Deadline: November 30 and April 30
Contact: Pat Williams, Director of Nursing, Division II

Florida State University Graduate Assistantship in Music *
School of Music
204D HMU R-71
Tallahassee, FL 32306-2098
(904) 644-4833

Description: Graduate scholarships for music majors
Restrictions: Limited to students majoring in a musical field
$ Given: 115 grants ranging $2,600-$6,000
Application Information: Write for guidelines.
Deadline: March 20
Contact: Dr. Jon Piersol, Associate Dean, School of Music

Florida State University The Madge Hutcherson Graduate Scholarship *
School of Library & Information Studies
101 Shores Building
Tallahassee, FL 32306-2048
(904) 644-8106

Description: Graduate scholarships for school library media specialists
Restrictions: Applicant must have undergraduate degree and have applied to the graduate program of the Florida State School of Library and Information Studies.
$ Given: $500- $5,000 each year
Application Information: Formal application is required.
Deadline: November 15
Contact: Dr. Mary Alice Hunt, Associate Dean

• • • • • • • • • • • • • • • • • • • •

Florida State University
School of Visual Arts
Master of Fine Arts
Program
Fellowships and
Assistantships *
School of Visual Arts
221 Fine Arts Building
Tallahassee, FL 32306-2037
APPLICATION ADDRESS:
Office of Financial Aid 127
Bryan Hall, Florida State
University (904) 644-6474

Description: Graduate fellowships and teaching
assistantships
Restrictions: Students in the School of Visual Arts
$ Given: Grants of $6,000-$10,000; assistantships of $2,600
plus $1,600 stipends
Application Information: Write for guidelines.
Deadlines: February 1
Contact: Gail Rubini, Chair, Graduate Program

Florida State University
State Farm Scholarship
College of Business
Department of Risk
Management
and Insurance
Room 313 RBA
Tallahassee, FL 32306

Description: Scholarships for business majors
Restrictions: Students must be studying the field of
business and must be nominated by the department head or
dean.
$ Given: 20 grants of $2,000 each
Application Information: Write for guidelines.
Deadline: February 28
Contact: the Department of Risk Management & Insurance

Florida State University
Society of Real Estate
Appraisers
Scholarships *
Student Aid Resource Center
Tallahassee, FL 32306
(904) 644-4840
APPLICATION ADDRESS:
Real Estate Department, 313
RBA (904) 644-4070

Description: Scholarships for college and/or graduate
students majoring in real estate
Restrictions: See above.
$ Given: 10 grants of $1,000 each
Application Information: Write for guidelines.
Deadline: November 2
Contact: Secretary, Real Estate Department

· ·

**Florida State University
School of Out-of-State
Tuition Waiver**
School of Theatre
328 Fine Arts Building
Tallahassee, FL 32306
(904) 644-5549

Description: Scholarships for honors theatre students and
students pursuing Bachelor of Fine Arts degrees
Restrictions: See above.
$ Given: 8 grants of $1,210-$1,368; average grant: $1,282
Application Information: Write for guidelines.
Deadline: January 31
Contact: James Thomas, Associate Dean

**Jacksonville University
Fine Arts Undergraduate
Scholarships**
College of Fine Arts
Jacksonville, FL 32211
(904) 744-3950

Description: Scholarships for talented students in music,
art, theatre or dance
Restrictions: See above.
$ Given: $24,000 over four years
Application Information: Formal application and audition
are required; submit portfolio.
Deadline: January 15
Contact: Dr. Thomas G. Owen, Dean

**Garth Reeves, Jr. Memorial
Scholarship for Students**
APPLICATION ADDRESS:
Bill Whiting,
c/o Miami Herald, Sigma
Delta Chi
Greater Miami Chapter
One Herald Plaza
Miami, FL 33101
(305) 350-2111

Description: Scholarships for minority journalism students
who are attending a college or university in the Miami area
Restrictions: See above.
$ Given: Varies
Application Information: Write for guidelines.
Deadline: February 1
Contact: Bill Whiting, Miami Herald

• • • • • • • • • • • • • • • • • • • •

**Reverend Donald
F.X. Connolly
WICI Scholarship**
Women in
Communications, Inc.
Greater Miami Chapter
P.O. Box 43-2641
South Miami, FL 33243

Description: Scholarships to female communication majors at University of Miami, Barry University, Miami-Dade Community College, University of Florida, University of South Florida and Florida State University
Restrictions: See above.
$ Given: Unspecified number of grants ranging $500-$1,000 each
Application Information: Write for guidelines.
Deadline: May
Contact: WICI, Greater Miami Chapter

**Rollins College
Priscilla Parker
Theatre Scholarship**
1000 Holt Avenue
Winter Park, FL 32789
(407) 646-2161
(407) 646-2501

Description: Renewable scholarships for freshmen theatre majors
Restrictions: Students must have at least a 3.0 GPA and show high grades and talent.
$ Given: 6 grants of $5,000 each
Application Information: Write for guidelines.
Deadline: March 1
Contact: Joseff Nasiff, Theatre Director

**Webber College
Athletic Scholarships**
P.O. Box 96
Babson Park, FL 33827
(813) 638-1431

Description: Athletic scholarships for undergraduates in the A.S. or B.S. program in Business Administration in men's golf and soccer, men's and women's basketball and tennis and in women's volleyball
Restrictions: Students must have at least a 2.0 GPA.
$ Given: 40 grants of $1,200; general range: $1,000- 1,500
Application Information: Write for guidelines.
Deadline: N/A
Contact: Joann McKenna, Director of Financial Aid

Webber College
Business Scholarship
P.O. Box 96
Babson Park, FL 33827
(813) 638-1431

Description: Scholarships for students who are majoring in business
Restrictions: Students must be recommended by their high school business departments, have a GPA of at least 2.75 and be residents of Polk or Highland counties, Florida.
$ Given: 3 grants of $1,000 each
Application Information: Interview is required.
Deadline: May 1
Contact: Joann McKenna, Director of Financial Aid

Webber College
Freshman Award
P.O. Box 96
Babson Park, FL 33827
(813) 638-1431

Description: Scholarships for first-year students in the A.S. or B.S. Business Administration Program
Restrictions: Student must be a resident of Florida.
$ Given: 35 awards of $1,000 each
Application Information: Write for guidelines.
Deadline: July 1
Contact: Joann McKenna, Director of Financial Aid

GEORGIA

Agnes Scott College
Nannette Hopkins Music
Scholarship
Music Department
Decatur, GA 30030
(404) 371-6000

Description: Scholarships for undergraduate music majors
Restrictions: See above.
$ Given: 4 grants of $2,000 each
Application Information: Auditions are required.
Deadline: January 15
Contact: Susan Little

Albany State College
Presidential Scholarship
Albany, GA 31705
(912) 430-4604

Description: Scholarships for freshmen
Restrictions: Students must maintain a 3.0 GPA.
$ Given: 10 grants of $4,500 each
Application Information: Write for guidelines.
Deadline: March 1
Contact: Billy C. Black, President

• • • • • • • • • • • • • • • • • • • •

Atlanta College of Art
School of Excellence Award
1280 Peachtree Street, NE
Atlanta, GA 30309
(800) 832-2104

Description: Scholarships for first-year undergraduates and transfer students
Restrictions: Students need recommendations from teachers in the art departments of their former schools.
$ Given: 71 grants of $1,000 each
Application Information: Write for guidelines.
Deadline: None
Contact: Teresa Tantillo, Director of Financial Aid

Atlanta University
Patricia Roberts Harris
Graduate Fellowships *
School of Library and
Information Studies 223
James P. Brawley Drive, SW
Atlanta, GA 30314
(404) 880-8694

Description: Graduate scholarships in library science
Restrictions: See above.
$ Given: 3 grants of $16,000
Application Information: Write for guidelines.
Deadline: March 1
Contact: Yvonne Chandler-Melvin, Assistant to the Dean of Special Projects

Berry College
Presidential Scholarship
Mount Berry Station
Rome, GA 30149
(404) 236-2244

Description: Scholarships for freshmen
Restrictions: Students must have high grades and test scores, as well as extra-curricular achievements.
$ Given: 10 grants of $3,000-$5,880 each
Application Information: Interview is required.
Deadline: February
Contact: Director of Admissions

Emory University
Alben W. Barkley
Debate Scholarship
Office of Admission
B. Jones Center
Atlanta, GA 30322
APPLICATION ADDRESS:
Drawer U, Emory University,
Atlanta, GA 30322

Description: Scholarships for students on the debate team who maintain high grades
Restrictions: See above.
$ Given: 2 grants ranging $2,000-$4,000 each
Application Information: Write for guidelines.
Deadline: March 1
Contact: Melissa Wade, Director of Forensics

• • • • • • • • • • • • • • • • • • • •

Emory University
Andrew W. Mellon Faculty
Fellowships in the
Humanities *
Mellon Fellowship
Committee
Emory University
Atlanta, GA 30322
(404) 727-0676

Description: Graduate fellowships for two years to research and teach in the Humanities
Restrictions: See above.
$ Given: Two-year stipend, research allowance and moving expenses
Application Information: Formal application is required; send resume, 500-word proposal and two letters of recommendation.
Deadline: N/A
Contact: Dean Irvin Hyatt, Fellowship Committee

Savannah College
of Art and Design
Georgia High School Art
Symposium Scholarship
Savannah College of Art
and Design
342 Bull Street
P.O. Box 3146
Savannah, GA
(912) 238-2400

Description: Renewable scholarships for freshmen who participate in the Georgia high school art exhibit symposium and who maintain at least a 3.0 GPA.
Restrictions: See above.
$ Given: 30 grants ranging $1,000- $10,000 each
Application Information: Write for guidelines.
Deadline: None
Contact: May Poetter, Dean of Admissions

Rosalone Turner/Margaret
Williams Memorial
Scholarships
Women in
Communications, Inc.
Georgia Chapter
APPLICATION ADDRESS:
Barbara Busey
204 Countryside Lane
Smyrna, GA 30080

Description: Scholarships for female undergraduates enrolled in a college in Georgia
Restrictions: See above.
$ Given: Grants of at least $500 each
Application Information: Write for guidelines.
Deadline: April
Contact: Barbara Busey

HAWAII

HAWAII

Ruth E. Black Scholarship Fund
American Association of University Women, Honolulu
1802 Keeaumoku Street
Honolulu, HI 96822
(808) 537-4702

Description: Scholarships for female residents in Hawaii enrolled in an university in Hawaii
Restrictions: See above.
$ Given: Unspecified number of grants $500-$1,000 each
Application Information: Write for guidelines.
Deadline: N/A
Contact: American Association University Women, Honolulu

East-West Center
East-West Center Scholarship and Fellowship Program *
1777 East-West Road
Honolulu, HI 96848
(808) 944-7735

Description: Funding for graduate students for program work at the University of Hawaii; for students taking a multi-disciplinary approach to problems of international concern in the areas of population, resource systems, environment, culture, and communication; recipients chosen on the basis of academic achievement and proposed course of study
Restrictions: U.S., Asian country, or Pacific Island citizenship required
$ Given: An unspecified number of grants awarded annually; each grant covers stipend, housing, medical insurance, travel, and university fees; supports up to 24 months of masters study, up to 48 months of PhD study
Application Information: Write for details
Deadline: Varies
Contact: Award Services Officer

Hawaii Loa College Hau'Mana Po'Okela Scholarship
45-045 Kamehameha Highway
Kaneohe
Oahu, HI 96744-5297
(808) 235-3641

Description: Scholarships for junior transfer students from community colleges
Restrictions: Transfer student must have 60 credits, and a 3.8 GPA.
$ Given: 4 grants of $2,500-$7,000; average range: $4,000
Application Information: Write for guidelines.
Deadline: April 30
Contact: Coleen Jongeward, Director of Financial Aid

• • • • • • • • • • • • • • • • • • •

Hawaii Loa College
High School Honor
Scholarship
45-045 Kamehameha
Highway
Kaneohe
Oahu, HI 96744-5297
(808) 235-3641

Description: Scholarships for freshmen
Restrictions: Must have combined SAT score of 1100 or ACT score of 20, rank in top 25% of class, and have at least a 3.6 GPA.
$ Given: 14 grants of $1,500 each
Application Information: Write for guidelines.
Deadlines: April 30
Contact: Coleen Jongeward, Director of Financial Aid

IDAHO

Paul Douglas Teacher
Scholarship
Idaho State Board of
Education
Len B. Jordan Building,
Room 307
650 West Side Street
Boise, ID 83720
(208) 334-2270

Description: Undergraduate scholarships for students pursuing a degree in education
Restrictions: Students must attend a university in Idaho, rank in top 10% of class and plan to teach for two years.
$ Given: 15 grants of $5,000 each
Application Information: Write for guidelines.
Deadline: February 15
Contact: Dolores Harris, Scholarship Assistant

Lewis-Clark State College
Minority and "At-Risk"
Scholarship
Financial Aid Office
Eighth Avenue and
Sixth Street
Lewiston, ID 83501
(208) 799-2210

Description: Scholarships for undergraduates
Restrictions: Limited to minority students residing in Idaho, who have a 2.5 GPA, are handicapped (as defined in 29 US code Section 794), or are immigrant farm workers.
$ Given: 2 grants of $2,500 each
Application Information: Write for guidelines.
Deadline: June 1
Contact: Financial Aid Office

ILLINOIS

Blackburn College
Honor Award
700 College Avenue
Carlinville, IL 62626
(217) 854-3231

Description: Scholarships for freshmen
Restrictions: Student must have high grades and maintain 3.0 GPA (2.8 first year).
$ Given: 82 grants of $1,000-$3,500; general range: $1,500
Application Information: Write for guidelines.
Deadline: None
Contact: John Malin, Admissions Director

DePaul University
Fritz A. Bauer Scholarship
25 East Jackson Boulevard
Suite 100
Chicago, IL 60654
(800) 433-7285

Description: Scholarships for first-year students in the College of Commerce/Business who ranked in the top 10% of their high school class
Restrictions: Students must plan to attend the College of Commerce, have a minimum ACT score of 27 or a SAT score of 1100, and a 3.3 GPA.
$ Given: 14 grants of $7,500
Application Information: Write for guidelines.
Deadline: February 1
Contact: Jennifer Sparrow, Scholarship Coordinator

DePaul University
Dean's Art Scholarship
25 East Jackson Boulevard
Suite 100
Chicago, IL 60604
(800) 433-7285

Description: Scholarships for art history or studio design majors
Restrictions: Students must have good grades, maintain a 2.5 GPA, and submit a portfolio containing 8-10 works.
$ Given: 11 grants ranging from $2,000-$7,000; average grant: $3,000
Application Information: Submit a portfolio as selection is based on talent.
Deadline: February 1
Contact: Jennifer Sparrow, Scholarship Coordinator

• • • • • • • • • • • • • • • • • • •

DePaul University
Dean's Science Scholarship
25 East Jackson Boulevard
Suite 100
Chicago, IL 60604

Description: Scholarships for freshmen interested in biology, chemistry or physics
Restrictions: Student must be in top 15% of class, have a ACT score of 26 or SAT of 1100 and maintain a 2.75 GPA.
$ Given: 50 grants of $2,000-$7,000; average range: $4,500
Application Information: Write for guidelines.
Deadline: February 1
Contact: Jennifer Sparrow, Scholarship Coordinator

DePaul University
Dean's Theatre Studies
Scholarship
25 East Jackson Boulevard
Suite 100
Chicago, IL 60604
(800) 433-7285

Description: Scholarships for freshmen majoring in theatre studies
Restrictions: Student must maintain at least a 2.75 GPA.
$ Given: 17 grants of $2,000-$6,000; average grant: $3,000
Application Information: Theatre admission interviews are required.
Deadline: February 1
Contact: Jennifer Sparrow, Scholarship Coordinator

Eureka College
Fine Arts Scholarship
300 East College
Eureka, IL 61530
(309) 467-6310

Description: Scholarships for freshmen
Restrictions: Students must maintain a 2.5 GPA and an interest in the fine arts.
$ Given: 6 grants ranging $1,000-$4,000; general range: $2,000
Application Information: Interview is required.
Deadline: May 1
Contact: Martin Stromberger, Director of Financial Aid

Illinois College
Presidential Scholarship
1101 West College Avenue
Jacksonville, IL 62650
(217) 245-3035

Description: Scholarships for undergraduates
Restrictions: Students must have a 3.0 GPA.
$ Given: 12 grants of $1,400 each
Application Information: Write for guidelines.
Deadline: June 1
Contact: N/A

**Loyola University of Chicago
First National Bank
Scholarship**
820 North Michigan Avenue
Chicago, IL 60611
(312) 670-3144

Description: Scholarships for business/management students
Restrictions: Students must be in the top 20% of their class and may apply only by the invitation of the dean.
$ Given: 1 grant of $4,000
Application Information: Write for guidelines.
Deadline: January 31
Contact: N/A

**Monmouth College
Performance Fellowship**
700 East Broadway
Monmouth, IL 61462
(309) 457-2129
(800) 747-2687

Description: Scholarships for freshmen with talent in art, music, theatre and creative writing
Restrictions: See above.
$ Given: 20 grants of $1,000 each
Application Information: Write for guidelines.
Deadline: N/A
Contact: Dr. David Long, Dean of Admissions

**Northwestern University
History and Philosophy of
Science Fellowships ***
Department of Philosophy
Evanston, IL 60208
(708) 491-3656

Description: Graduate scholarships for students of history, philosophy, and social studies of science
Restrictions: Must have a B.A.
$ Given: $7,803
Application Information: Write for guidelines.
Deadline: January 15
Contact: Dr. David L. Hull, Philosophy Department

**School of the Art
Institute of Chicago
Presidential Scholarship**
37 South Wabash Avenue
Chicago, IL 60603
(312) 899-5100

Description: Scholarships for undergraduates
Restrictions: Student must have a 3.0 GPA and artistic skills.
$ Given: Up to 10 grants ranging $3,720- $4,650
Application Information: Write for guidelines.
Deadline: March 15
Contact: Tim Robison, Director of Admissions Office

. . . .

**University of Illinois,
Urbana-Champaign
The Kate Neal Kinley
Memorial Fellowship ***
Kinley Fellowship Committee
College of Fine &
Applied Arts
110 Architecture Building
608 East Lorado Taft Drive
Champaign, IL 61820
(217) 333-1661

Description: Graduate scholarships for study in art, music or architecture
Restrictions: Students must be graduates of the College of Fine & Applied Arts at University of Illinois, Urbana-Champaign.
$ Given: 2 fellowships of $7,000
Application Information: Write for guidelines
Deadline: March 15
Contact: Kinley Fellowship Committee

INDIANA

**Eisenhower
Memorial Graduate
Scholarships
Indiana University ***
Eisenhower Memorial
Scholarship Foundation
303 North Curry Pike
Bloomington, IN 47404-2502

Description: Graduate scholarships
Restrictions: Students must have received their B.A. from Indiana University or at Hillsdale College in Michigan.
$ Given: $1,000- $3,000
Application Information: Formal application is required.
Deadline: February 1
Contact: E.M. Sears, Executive Director

**DePauw University
Charles Grannon
Scholarship**
Greencastle, IN 46135
(317) 658-4000
APPLICATION ADDRESS:
Center for Management &
Entrepreneurship L-30 East
College, DePauw University,
Greencastle, IN 46135
(317) 658-4024

Description: Scholarships for first-year students in the management fellows program
Restrictions: Students must maintain a 3.4 GPA in order to renew award.
$ Given: 3 awards of $4,000 each
Application Information: Write for guidelines.
Deadline: February 15
Contact: Thomas Boese, Director

· ·

Earlham College
Honors Scholarship
Richmond, IN 47374
(317) 983-1200

Description: Scholarships for freshmen
Restrictions: Students must have high grades,
SAT scores of 1100 or ACT of 26.
$ Given: 10 grants of $2,500 for four years
Application Information: Submit a sample of scholastic
or creative work; interviews are required.
Deadline: February 15
Contact: Robert de Veer, Dean of Admissions

Franklin College
Pulliam Journalism
Scholarship
501 East Monroe Street
Franklin, IN 46131
(317) 736-8441

Description: Scholarships for first-year undergraduates with
an interest in journalism
Restrictions: Student must maintain a 3.0 GPA.
$ Given: 63 grants of $2,100; general range: $2,000-$12,000
Application Information: Write for guidelines.
Deadline: December 15
Contact: Sarah Poynter, Associate Director of Financial Aid

Indiana University
Jane Addams
Philanthropy Fellowships *
Indiana University Center
for Philanthropy
550 West North Street
Suite 301
Indianapolis, IN 46202-3162
(317) 274-4200

Description: Graduate fellowships for the study and practice
of philanthropy
Restrictions: Must have undergraduate degree not more
than three years before applying, and an interest in
philanthropy.
$ Given: $15,000 and tuition for one year
Application Information: Write for guidelines.
Deadline: March 15
Contact: University Center for Philanthropy

Indiana University
Myrna L. Bernath
History Fellowship *
Department of History
Ballantine Hall 742
Bloomington, IN 47405

Description: Graduate scholarships for research and study
Restrictions: Female students who want to do historically-based research at University or abroad
$ Given: $2,500
Application Information: Submit 3 copies of 15-page typed proposal and three references.
Deadline: November 30
Contact: Joan Hoff, Society for History American Foreign Relations

Indiana University
Concortium for Graduate
Study in Management
Fellowships *
APPLICATION ADDRESS: c/o
Ms. Jackie Moll Hampton
Suite 616, South Hanley Road
St. Louis, Missouri 63105
(314) 935-6353

Description: Graduate scholarships for minority men and women pursuing degrees in business management
Restrictions: Students must have B.A. degree and have taken the GMAT exam.
$ Given: 160-175 fellowships of $2,500 each plus 2 years tuition
Application Information: Write for guidelines.
Deadline: February 1
Contact: Ms. Jackie Moll Hampton at above address

Indiana University
Library & Information
Science Fellowships *
School of Library & Life
Science
Indiana University
Bloomington, IN 47405

Description: One-year fellowships to support students in their masters degree or doctorate program in library sciences.
Restrictions: See above.
$ Given: Up to 3 years paid graduate study
Application Information: Send letter of interest.
Deadline: N/A
Contact: Mary Krutulis, Director Admissions or Dr. Daniel Callison, Associate Dean

INDIANA

Indiana University
School of Fine Arts
Graduate Fellowships *
Indiana University
Fine Arts Building, Room 123
Bloomington, IN 47405
(818) 855-0188

Description: Graduate scholarships for students in the Fine Arts Program
Restrictions: See above.
$ Given: N/A
Application Information: Write for application.
Deadline: February 1
Contact: Graduate Secretary, School of Fine Arts

Tri-State University
Lincoln Scholarship
South Darling
Angola, IN 46703
(219) 665-4175

Description: Scholarship for a minority student who is majoring in business or computer science
Restrictions: Minority student must be from Allen County.
$ Given: $5,000
Application Information: Write for guidelines.
Deadline: March 1
Contact: N/A

University of
Indianapolis
Music Grant *
1400 East Hanna Avenue
Indianapolis, IN 46227
(317) 788-3217

Description: Scholarships for undergraduates and graduate students majoring in music
Restrictions: See above.
$ Given: 10 grants ranging $1,000-3,000; general range: $1,500
Application Information: Auditions are required.
Deadline: N/A
Contact: Rita S. Hankley, Assistant Director of Financial Aid

University of
Southern Indiana
Presidential Scholarship
8600 University Boulevard
Evansville, IN 47712
(812) 464-1877

Description: Scholarships for high school valedictorians or salutatorians with SAT scores of 1000
Restrictions: Students must maintain a 3.2 GPA first year, a 3.4 thereafter.
$ Given: 50 grants of $1,200-$4,600; general range: $2,990
Application Information: Write for guidelines.
Deadline: March 1
Contact: Timothy Buecher, Director of Admissions

• •

**University of
Southern Indiana
Robert and Elaine Pott
Scholarship**
8600 University Boulevard
Evansville, IN 47712
(812) 464-1877

Description: Undergraduate scholarships for engineering
students and transfer students
Restrictions: Students must have a SAT score of 1000, and
maintain a 3.0 GPA.
$ Given: 26 grants of $1,600 each.
Application Information: Write for guidelines.
Contact: Augustine J. Fredrich, Chairman of Engineering
Technology

**Wabash College
Fine Arts Fellowship**
301 West Wabash Avenue
Crawfordsville, IN 47933
(317) 362-1400

Description: Scholarships for freshmen
Restrictions: Students must maintain a 3.0 GPA.
$ Given: 2 grants ranging $6,900-$8,625
Application Information: Write for guidelines.
Deadline: February 3
Contact: Greg Birk, Admissions Director

IOWA

**Ball State University
Presidential In-State
Scholarship**
Office of Scholarships
and Financial Aid
2000 University Avenue, AD 202
Muncie, IN 47306
(317) 285-5600

Description: Scholarships for freshmen
Restrictions: Must be resident of Indiana, rank in top 20% of
class, have SAT score of 1030 or ACT score of 23, and
maintain a 3.0 GPA.
$ Given: 284 awards of $1,528 each
Application Information: Write for guidelines.
Deadline: February 1
Contact: John H. Starnes, Associate Director of Scholarships

• • • • • • • • • • • • • • • • • • • •

Central College
Robertson Science
Scholarship
812 University Avenue
Pella, IA 50219
(800) 458-5503

Description: Scholarship for freshmen majoring in Natural Sciences
Restrictions: Students must be in top 10% of their high school class and maintain 3.0 GPA.
$ Given: 2 grants of $5,500
Application Information: Write for guidelines.
Deadline: January 1
Contact: Eric D. Sickler, Director of Admissions

Central College
Petz Scholarship
in Business and
International Studies
812 University Avenue
Pella, IA 50219
(800) 458-5503

Description: Scholarships for freshmen
Restrictions: Student must be interested in a career in international business, be in top 10% of class and maintain a 3.0 GPA.
$ Given: 2 grants of $5,500
Application Information: Write for guidelines.
Deadline: January 1
Contact: Eric D. Sickler, Admissions Director

Cornell College
Dugan Art Scholarship
Mount Vernon, IA 52314

Description: Scholarships for freshman
Restrictions: Students need an art portfolio and to participate in an art show.
$ Given: 4 grants of $2,000
Application Information: Write for guidelines.
Deadline: February 1
Contact: Kevin Crockett, Assistant Director of Admissions and Financial Aid

• •

Iowa Broadcasters Association Scholarship in Broadcast Journalism
Iowa Broadcasters
Association
P.O. Box 2819
417 First Avenue
Cedar Rapids, IA 52406
(316) 366-8016

Description: Undergraduate scholarships for journalism majors attending Drake University, Iowa State University or the University of Iowa.
Restrictions: Students must maintain academic standards.
$ Given: 2 grants of $2,500 each
Application Information: Include class rank, GPA, and career plans.
Deadline: April 1
Contact: N/A

Iowa Press Women Scholarship
Iowa Press Women, Inc.
APPLICATION ADDRESS:
Jane Whitmore
2005 8th Street
Emmetsburg, IA 50536
(712) 852-2568

Description: Scholarships for undergraduates interested in journalism
Restrictions: Junior female communications students at Iowa State University, University of Iowa, or Drake University who are in top 50% of class
$ Given: Grants of $750
Application Information: Write for guidelines.
Deadline: N/A
Contact: Jane Whitmore

Iowa State University Freda Huncke Award
Department of English
Ames, IA 50011
(515) 294-3457

Description: Scholarships for English majors
Restrictions: Students must demonstrate writing skills and have high grades.
$ Given: 5 grants of $1,000 each.
Application Information: Write for guidelines.
Deadline: March 31
Contact: English Department

• •

Iowa State University
Freshman Engineering
Scholarship
College of Engineering
101 Marston Hall
Ames, IA 50011
(515) 294-1003

Description: Scholarships for engineering majors
Restrictions: Students must have high grades and SAT scores.
$ Given: 15 grants of $1,000 each
Application Information: Write for guidelines.
Deadline: July 15
Contact: College of Engineering

Iowa State University
John Vincent Atanasoff
Fellowship
Department of
Computer Science *
Ames, IA 50011
(515) 294-4377

Description: Scholarship for computer science major
Restrictions: Must be a second-year graduate student at Iowa State.
$ Given: 1 grant of $14,000
Application Information: Write for guidelines.
Deadline: March 1
Contact: Computer Science Department

Iowa State University
Scholarship for Excellence
Financial Aid and Student
Employment Office
12 Beardshear Hall
Ames, IA 50011
(515) 294-2243
(515) 294-0063

Description: Scholarships for first year undergraduates attending Iowa State University
Restrictions: Students must rank in top 20% of h.s. class, maintain a 3.0 G.P.A. at Iowa State and have interests in agriculture.
$ Given: 10 awards of $2,500 each
Application Information: Write for guidelines.
Deadline: October 31
Contact: Ardys Ulrichson, Scholarship Coordinator

University of Iowa
Iowa Center for the
Arts Scholarship
Iowa City, IA 52240
(319) 353-2121
APPLICATION ADDRESS:
Admissions Office, 108 Calvin
Hall IC (319) 335-1497

Description: Scholarships for university freshmen
Restrictions: Students need auditions or portfolio reviews.
$ Given: 4 grants of $2,500 each
Application Information: Write for guidelines; auditions required.
Deadline: Varies
Contact: Janet Ashman, Assistant Director of Admissions

. . . .

Wartburg College
Regents Scholarship
222 Ninth Street, NW
Waverly, IA 50677
(319) 352-8262

Description: Scholarships for freshmen
Restrictions: Students must rank in top 10% of class, have
3.0 GPA and a 28 ACT score.
$ Given: 600 awards ranging $2,500-$8,000,
general range: $3,000
Application Information: Write for guidelines.
Deadline: December 1
Contact: J.F. Nugent, Director of Admissions

KANSAS

Baker University
Scholar Award
Eighth and Grove
Baldwin City, KS 66006
(913) 594-6451

Description: Scholarships for freshmen
Restrictions: Student must take an exam, show leadership
ability and attend a campus seminar held in February.
$ Given: 5 grants of $4,400
Application Information: Interview, campus visit and
recommendations are required.
Deadline: February
Contact: Director of Financial Aid

Benedictine College
Academic Scholarship
Second and Division
Atchison, KS 66002
(913) 367-5340

Description: Scholarships for freshmen
Restrictions: Student must maintain a 3.0 GPA
$ Given: 145 grants of $1,600-$5,800; general range: $1,900
Application Information: Submit financial aid application;
write for guidelines.
Deadline: March 1
Contact: Jim Hoffman, Dean of Enrollment Management

Bethany College Award
421 North First Street
Lindsborg, KS 67456-1897
(913) 223-3311

Description: Scholarships for undergraduates
Restrictions: Student must have an ACT score of 21, a 3.0 GPA and maintain a 2.75 GPA.
$ Given: 114 awards of $1,600-$2,200; general range: $1,700
Application Information: Write for guidelines.
Deadline: N/A
Contact: Jayne Norlin, Director Financial Aid

Bethel College
Presidential Scholarship
Financial Aid Office
North Newton, KS 67117
(316) 283-2500

Description: Scholarships for freshmen
Restrictions: Student must show high grades, artistic or athletic ability and maintain a 3.2 GPA.
$ Given: 25 grants of $2,000 each
Application Information: Write for guidelines.
Deadline: None
Contact: Daniel C. Nelson, Director of College Financial Planning

Emporia State University
Woodruff Scholarship
1200 Commercial
Emporia. KS 66801-5087
(316) 343-5457

Description: Scholarships for freshmen with leadership skills
Restrictions: Student must have high ACT scores, be in top 20% of class.
$ Given: 3 grants of $3,000 each
Application Information: Write for guidelines; interview on campus is suggested.
Deadline: February 15
Contact: Wilma D. Kasnic, Director of Student Financial Aid

Fort Hays State University
Art Department Graduate
Assistantships *
600 Park Street
Hays, KS 67601

Description: Graduate assistantships for students in the Department of Art
Restrictions: Students must have a B.A. or B.F.A. in art.
$ Given: Grants of $3,270
Application Information: Write for guidelines.
Deadline: March 1
Contact: Chairperson, Department of Art

• • • • • • • • • • • • • • • • • • • •

Ottawa University
President's Scholarship
Ottawa, KS 66067
(913) 242-5200

Description: Scholarships for undergraduates
Restrictions: Students must rank in top 5% of class, and have a 25 ACT score.
$ Given: 6 grants ranging from $1,000-$1,500
Application Information: Write for guidelines; interview is required.
Deadline: N/A
Contact: University Financial Aid Office

University of Kansas
Harold E. Fellows
Memorial Scholarship
National Association of
Broadcasters
University of Kansas
Stauffer-Flint Hall
Lawrence, KS 66045

Description: Scholarships for undergraduates
Restrictions: Parents of student applicant must be affiliated with the National Association of Broadcasters and have worked for a broadcasting station.
$ Given: 4 grants of $1,250 each
Application Information: Write for guidelines.
Deadline: January 31
Contact: N/A

University of Kansas
Speech Language
Pathology & Audiology
Training Fellowships *
3031 Dole
Department of Speech,
Language
and Hearing
Lawrence, KS 66045
(913) 864-0630

Description: Graduate scholarships in communicative disorders
Restrictions: Students must be enrolled in the University Intercampus Graduate Program in Communicative Disorders.
$ Given: $5,000 ($500 per month for 10 months)
Application Information: Write for guidelines.
Deadline: February 15
Contact: Hugh Catts, PhD, Admissions Chair

• • • • • • • • • • • • • • • • • • •

KENTUCKY

Bellarmine College
President's Scholarship
Newburg Road
Louisville, KY 40205
(502) 452-8131

Description: Scholarships for freshmen
Restrictions: Student must demonstrate leadership skills
$ Given: 33 grants of $2,600- $4,500; general range: $3,425
Application Information: On-site interview is suggested
Deadline: March 15
Contact: Robert Pfaadt, Registrar

Campbellsville College
Academic Scholarship
200 West College Street
Campbellsville, KY 42718

Description: Scholarships for freshmen
Restrictions: Students must have ACT score of 22 or SAT score of 900 and a 3.25 GPA
$ Given: 100 grants of $2,095-$6,900 each
Application Information: Write for guidelines.
Deadline: N/A
Contact: Philip Hanna, Director of Admissions

Centre College
Trustee Scholarship
West Walnut Street
Danville, KY 40422
(606) 236-5211

Description: Scholarships for freshmen
Restrictions: Student must have high grades, leadership skills and maintain a 3.2 GPA.
$ Given: 20 grants of $6,000 each
Application Information: Write for guidelines.
Deadline: February 1
Contact: Tom McKune, Director of Admissions

Thomas More College
Presidential Scholarship
333 Thomas More Parkway
Crestview Hills, KY 41017
(606) 344-3331

Description: Scholarships for undergraduates
Restrictions: Students must show financial needs and maintain a 3.0 GPA.
$ Given: 90 grants of $1,000-$5,000; general range: $1,904
Application Information: Write for guidelines.
Deadline: March 15
Contact: Paul Calme, Director of Financial Aid

Murray State University
Graduate Assistantships
in Art *
Price Doyle Fine Arts Center
FA 404
Murray, KY 42071
(502) 762-3784

Description: Graduate assistantships
Restrictions: Must be graduate students majoring in art
$ Given: $3,600 plus out-of-state tuition waiver
Application Information: Include resume, portfolio and letters of recommendation.
Deadline: April 15
Contact: Melody Weiler, Chair, Department of Art

University of Kentucky
Scott Memorial Scholarship
127 Funkhouser Building
Lexington, KY 40506
(606) 257-3172

Description: Scholarships for female undergraduates
Restrictions: Student must be female, be in top 20% of class, and live in Kentucky.
$ Given: 2 grants of $2,000 each
Application Information: Write for guidelines.
Deadline: April 1
Contact: N/A

LOUISIANA

Centenary
College of Louisiana
Church Careers Scholarship
2911 Centenary Boulevard
Shreveport, LA 71104
(318) 869-5137

Description: Scholarship grants for undergraduates contemplating church careers
Restrictions: Must be accepted into the Church Careers Program.
$ Given: 71 grants of $1,000 each
Application Information: Write for guidelines.
Deadline: March 15
Contact: Mary Sue Rix, Director of Financial Aid

Centenary
College of Louisiana
Minister's Dependent
Scholarship
2911 Centenary Boulevard
Shreveport, LA 71104
(318) 869-5137

Description: Scholarship grants for undergraduates
Restrictions: Must be the dependent of a minister in the Louisiana Conference of the United Methodist Church.
$ Given: 15 grants of $1,350 each
Application Information: Write for guidelines.
Deadline: March 15
Contact: Mary Sue Rix, Director of Financial Aid.

• • • • • • • • • • • • • • • • • • •

**McNeese State University
H.C. Drew Manual Training
Scholarship**
McNeese State University
Scholarship and
Testing Service
P.O. Box 92575
Lake Charles, LA 70609-2575
(318) 475-5140

Description: Scholarship grants for undergraduates
Restrictions: See above.
$ Given: 100 grants of $1,000 each
Application Information: Write for guidelines.
Deadline: N/A
Contact: Financial Aid Office

**McNeese State University
Professional High
Proficiency Scholarship
and Testing Service**
P.O. Box 92575
Lake Charles, LA 70609-2575
(318) 475-5140

Description: Scholarship grants for sophomores, juniors,
and seniors studying pharmacy
Restrictions: Must be a full-time student with a minimum
3.2 GPA.
$ Given: 90 grants of $1,000 each
Application Information: Write for guidelines.
Deadline: N/A
Contact: Dee Berkey, Director of Financial Aid

**McNeese State University
The William T. and Ethel
Lewis Burton Foundation**
One Lakeshore Drive
Suite 1700
Lake Charles, LA 70629

Description: Scholarship grants for members of the
McNeese State University football team
Restrictions: Must be a member of the McNeese State
University football team and must maintain a minimum
2.5 GPA.
$ Given: Total giving of $319,385
Application Information: Write for guidelines.
Deadline: N/A
Contact: William P. Lawton, Chairman

**Southeastern
Louisiana University
Board of Trustees
Academic Scholarship**
Honors Program Office
P.O. Box 489
University Station
Hammond, LA 70402
(504) 549-2135

Description: Scholarship grants for unspecified
undergraduates
Restrictions: Must be a Louisiana high school graduate with
a minimum ACT score of 20 and a minimum high school
GPA of 3.0.
$ Given: 25 awards of $1,700 each
Application Information: Write for guidelines
Deadline: February
Contact: N/A

. . . .

Southeastern
Louisiana University
Education Majors Program
Department of Education
P.O. Box 94064
Baton Rouge, LA 70804-9064

Description: Scholarship grants for undergraduates studying Education
Restrictions: Must be a graduate of the Louisiana public school system or of an approved private high school, have a minimum 3.0 GPA and a minimum ACT of 22, maintain a 3.0 GPA and a minimum of 12 hours/semester.
$ Given: 20 awards of $2,000 each
Application Information: Write for guidelines
Deadline: December 1
Contact: N/A

Southeastern
Louisiana University
Paul Douglas Scholarship
Governor's Special
Commission on
Education, Services
P.O. Box 44127
Capitol Station
Baton Rouge, LA 70804

Description: Scholarship grants for undergraduates studying Education
Restrictions: Must be a graduate of the Louisiana public school system or of an approved private high school, and have a minimum 3.0 GPA and a minimum ACT of 22.
$ Given: 7 grants of up to $5,000 each
Application Information: Write for guidelines.
Deadline: December 1
Contact: N/A

MAINE

Saint Joseph's College
Student Leadership Award
White's Bridge Rd.
North Windham, ME 04062
(207) 892-6766

Description: Scholarship grants for freshmen
Restrictions: Must meet 2 of the following criteria: minimum combined 1000 SAT, rank in top 10% of high school class, be a member of National Honor Society, or demonstrate leadership ability.
$ Given: 7 grants of $2,000-$7,800 each
Application Information: Write for guidelines.
Deadline: March 15
Contact: Andrea Cross, Director of Financial Aid

MAINE

• • • • • • • • • • • • • • • • • • • •

Thomas College
Maine High School
Teachers Scholarship
180 West River Rd.
Waterville, ME 04901-9986
(207) 877-0101

Description: Scholarship grants for freshmen
Restrictions: Must be a resident of Maine, be nominated by a Maine high school teacher, show academic achievement, and leadership potential and social responsibility
$ Given: 10 grants of $7,300 each
Application Information: Write for guidelines.
Deadline: January 27
Contact: David Thombs, Director of College Scholarships

Thomas College
Trustee's Scholarship
180 West River Road
Waterville, ME 04901-9986
(207) 877-0101

Description: Scholarship grants for undergraduates
Restrictions: Must demonstrate need and academic achievement.
$ Given: 200 grants of $1,000 each
Deadline: February 1
Contact: N/A

MARYLAND

Frostburg State University
Paul Douglas Teacher
Scholarship
Frostburg State University
Foundation, Inc.
Frostburg, MD 21532
(301) 689-4000

Description: Scholarship grants for undergraduates studying Education
Restrictions: Must be enrolled full-time in a teacher certification program. The student must also be a Maryland resident and rank in the top tenth of class.
$ Given: Maximum grant of $5,000
Application Information: Write for guidelines.
Deadline: March 31
Contact: Katherine M. Kutler, Director of Financial aid

• • • • • • • • • • • • • • • • • • • •

Maryland Institute College of Art Fanny Thalheimer Scholarship
1300 West Mt. Royal Ave.
Baltimore, MD 21217
(301) 669-9200

Description: Scholarship grants for high school seniors planning to enter the Institute as freshmen following graduation
Restrictions: Selection is based on the quality of artwork and academic achievement of the applicant.
$ Given: 30 grants ranging from $5,000-$25,000.
Application Information: Write for guidelines.
Deadline: March 1
Contact: N/A

Maryland Institute College of Art Maryland Institute College of Art Fellowship Grants *
1300 West Mt. Royal Ave.
Baltimore, MD 21217
(301) 669-9200

Description: Scholarship grants for tuition for painting and sculpture studio programs leading to the MFA degree
Restrictions: Must have a BA or BFA degree with at least 40 studio credits and 6 art history credits.
$ Given: Varies
Application Information: Write for guidelines.
Deadline: March 1
Contact: N/A

University of Maryland American Society of Heating, Refrigeration, and Air Conditioning Scholarship
College of Engineering
College Park, MD 20742
(301) 405-3878

Description: Scholarship grants for African-American, Hispanic, or Native American engineering students
Restrictions: Must be a sophomore with a minimum 3.0 GPA, which must be maintained.
$ Given: 2 grants of $2,500-$6,000 each.
Application Information: Write for guidelines.
Deadline: December 15
Contact: Rosemary L. Parker, Director

• •

University of Maryland Benjamin Scholarship for Study of International Education*
Harold R. W. Benjamin International Scholarship Review Committee
College of Education
Benjamin Bldg.
Rm. 2110
College Park, MD 20742

Description: Scholarship grants for graduate study of international aspects of education
Restrictions: See above.
$ Given: Stipend of $3,000 per year, graduate assistantship of $9,100-$10,200 per year, and waiver of tuition charges for 10 graduate credit hours per semester.
Application Information: Write for guidelines.
Deadline: April 30
Contact: N/A

University of Maryland College of Journalism High School Senior Scholarship
College of Journalism
College Park, MD 20742
(301) 454-0100

Description: A four-year scholarship grant for an outstanding Maryland high school print journalist
Restrictions: Must attend a Maryland high school and plan to study journalism as a freshman at the University of Maryland.
$ Given: $10,000
Application Information: Write for guidelines.
Deadline: March 1
Contact: N/A

University of Maryland Creative/Performing Arts Scholarship
Division of Arts and Humanities
1101 Francis Scott Key
College Park, MD 20742
(301) 454-6803

Description: Scholarship grants for outstanding freshmen and transfers
Restrictions: Must be in the fields of art, music, dance, or theatre.
$ Given: 60 grants of $2,100 each
Application Information: Write for guidelines.
Deadline: March 1
Contact: N/A

• • • • • • • • • • • • • • • • • • •

University of Maryland
Education Policy, Planning,
and Administration
Doctoral Assistantships *
Department of Education
Policy, Planning,
and Administration
Benjamin Bldg.
Rm. 2110
College Park, MD 20742
(301) 454-5424

Description: Scholarship grants in the form of assistantships for graduate students in educational administration, curriculum theory and development, education policy, higher education, and social foundations of education
Restrictions: Must be accepted to the University of Maryland first.
$ Given: $9,000 assistantship and tuition for 10 graduate credit hours
Application Information: Submit a statement of academic goals, transcripts, test scores, and name 3 faculty references with addresses and phone numbers.
Deadline: February 24
Contact: Donald Warren, Chair

Washington College
Beneficial-Hodson
Trust Scholarship
Chestertown, MD 21620
(301) 778-2800

Description: Scholarship grants for undergraduates
Restrictions: Student must be nominated by own school counselor.
$ Given: 14 awards of $2,000 each
Application Information: Write for guidelines.
Deadline: March 15
Contact: N/A

MASSACHUSETTS

Amherst College
Centennial Educational
Trust Fund
Shawmut Bank of Hampshire
County
Amherst, MA 01022
(413) 256-5511

Description: Scholarship grants for seniors
Restrictions: See above.
$ Given: 6 grants of $3,000 each
Application Information: Write for guidelines.
Deadline: June 1
Contact: Robert J. Coleman

MASSACHUSETTS

• •

**Boston College
at Chestnut Hill
Monsignor George V. Kerr
Scholarship Trust**
P.O. Box 44
North Adams, MA 01220
(413) 458-8057

Description: Scholarship grant for undergraduates
Restrictions: See above.
$ Given: $2,000
Application Information: Submit an essay explaining academic qualifications and send current college transcript.
Deadline: N/A
Contact: Edward MacDonald, Trustee

**Brandeis University
Irving and Rose
Scholarships and
Fellowships in History of
American Civilization ***
Department of History
Olin-Sang 215
Waltham, MA 02254-9110

Description: Scholarship grants for graduate study and research leading to a PhD in American History, with related studies in comparative European history and in a field of humanities or social sciences
Restrictions: Must have a BA, MA, or professional training, preferably with a strong background in history, American studies, or related fields. Applicants must be seeking a PhD.
$ Given: A maximum grant of $8,500 and full tuition renewable through 4 years
Application Information: Write for guidelines.
Deadline: March 1
Contact: David Hackett Fischer, Chair, Graduate Program in American Civilization, Department of History

**Clark University
Worcester County
Alumni Scholarship**
950 Main Street
Worcester, MA 01610
(508) 793-7478

Description: Scholarship grants for freshmen
Restrictions: Must be a graduate of a Worcester County high school or a resident of Worcester County and must demonstrate financial need.
$ Given: 29 grants ranging from $1,000-$12,900.
Application Information: Write for guidelines.
Deadline: February 15
Contact: Betsy Astolei, Alumni Admissions Coordinator

Emerson College
RKO General Inc.
Minority Scholarship
100 Beacon Street
Boston, MA 02116
(617) 578-8655

Description: Scholarship grants for minority students majoring or intending to major in an area of communications to the public (film, radio, television, or print/broadcast journalism).
Restrictions: Students must be residents of Massachusetts and belong to one of the following ethnic groups: African-American, American Indian, Alaskan native, Asian, Pacific Islander, or Hispanic. Must be in good standing academically at all times. Preference is given to those who demonstrate financial need.
$ Given: 15 grants of $1,000 each
Application Information: Write for guidelines.
Deadline: April 1
Contact: N/A

Hampshire College
Centennial Educational
Trust Fund
Shawmut Bank of
Hampshire County
Amherst, MA 01022
(413) 256-5511

Description: Scholarship grants for seniors
Restrictions: See above.
$ Given: 6 grants of $3,000 each
Application Information: Write for guidelines.
Deadline: June 1
Contact: Robert J. Coleman

Harvard University
The Academy
Scholars Program *
The Center for
International Affairs
1737 Cambridge St.
Cambridge, MA 02138
(617) 495-2137

Description: Scholarship grants for doctoral candidates-PhD or comparable professional school degree-and recent recipients of these degrees
Restrictions: See above
$ Given: Depends on individual circumstances. Stipend from $20,000-$22,000 per year for predoctoral students and from $30,000-$35,000 for postdoctoral recipients, 4-6 grants are available per year.
Application Information: Write for guidelines.
Deadline: October 15
Contact: Christopher Briggs-Hale

MASSACHUSETTS

Harvard University
Charles J. Paine
Scholarship Fund Trust
c/o Taylor, Granson & Perrin
160 Franklin St.
Boston, MA 02110
(617) 951-2777

Description: Scholarship grants for undergraduates
Restrictions: See above.
$ Given: 6 grants of $1,500-$3,500
Application Information: Must submit an initial letter describing financial need and biographical information.
Deadline: N/A
Contact: Charles M. Granson, Jr., Trustee

Harvard University
George S. Dively
Fellowships in Business
and Government *
79 John F. Kennedy St.
Belfer 503
Cambridge, MA 02138
(617) 495-1446

Description: Scholarship grants for graduate students enrolled in established programs in business and government
Restrictions: Must conduct research consistent with the mission of the Center for Business and Government.
$ Given: $5,000
Application Information: Write for guidelines.
Deadline: N/A
Contact: Prof. John T. Dunlop, Center for Business and Government, John F. Kennedy School of Government

Harvard University
Grace T. Blanchard Trust
f/b/o Flora T. Blanchard
Scholarships
c/o Easton Bank &
Trust Company
225 Essex Street
Salem, MA 01970-3728
(617) 599-2100

Description: Scholarship grants for Massachusetts residents
Restrictions: See above.
$ Given: $2,000
Application Information: Write for guidelines.
Deadline: N/A
Contact: Gary A. Petersen

Harvard University
Harvard Academy for
International and Area
Studies Fellowships *
The Center for
International Affairs
1737 Cambridge St.
Cambridge, MA 02138

Description: Scholarship grants for both Harvard and non-Harvard PhD candidates and recent recipients
Restrictions: Must specialize in area studies.
$ Given: Grants of $20,000-$25,000 for predoctoral candidates and $30,000-$35,000 for postdoctoral candidates, health insurance and university facilities fees are also provided.
Application Information: Write for guidelines.
Deadline: October
Contact: Christopher Briggs-Hale

Harvard University
Harvard MacArthur
Scholarships in
International Affairs *
Center for
International Affairs
1737 Cambridge St.
Cambridge, MA 02138
(617) 495-9899

Description: Scholarship grants for Harvard PhD candidates
Restrictions: Must study international security.
$ Given: Approximately 10 grants of $14,000 each plus individual health insurance and university facilities fees
Application Information: Write for guidelines.
Deadline: February 5
Contact: Jean Shildneck, Committee on International Security

Harvard University
International Institutions
Pre- and Postdoctoral
Fellowships *
The Center for
International Affairs
1737 Cambridge St.
Cambridge, MA 02138
(617) 495-9899

Description: Scholarship grants for Harvard and non-Harvard PhD candidates or recent recipients working on research of international institutions, tenable at Harvard for 1 academic year.
Restrictions: Must focus on problems of international institutions.
$ Given: 2-4 awards, $14,000 for predoctoral and $24,000 for postdoctoral candidates, grants also include costs of individual health insurance and university facilities.
Application Information: Write for guidelines.
Deadline: February
Contact: Jean Shildneck, Fellowships Coordinator

MASSACHUSETTS

**Harvard University
K T Li Predoctoral
Fellowship on the Newly
Industrialized Countries ***
The Center for
International Affairs
1737 Cambridge St.
Cambridge, MA 02138
(617) 495-8292

Description: Scholarship grants for graduate students at Harvard University
Restrictions: Research must concentrate on Taiwan, South Korea, Hong Kong, or Singapore. Preference is given to students with some East Asian language ability.
$ Given: 2 grants of $10,000 each
Application Information: Write for guidelines.
Deadline: March
Contact: Jean Shildneck, Fellowships Coordinator

**Harvard Academy for
International and
Area Studies
Scholars Program ***
Center for
International Affairs
420 Coolidge Hall
1737 Cambridge Street
Cambridge, MA 02138
(617) 495-2137 or
(617) 495-9498

Description: Grants for doctoral candidates at dissertation level and recent PhDs to conduct research in several fields, including area and cultural studies, demography and population studies, economics, geography, history, languages, literatures and linguistics, political science and public policy, psychology, sociology, anthropology, archaeology, law, international affairs, and interdisciplinary programs in the humanities and social sciences; recipients chosen on the basis of academic achievement and proposed research
Restrictions: Young applicants preferred; preference to individuals pursuing academic careers involving social science disciplines as relevant to specific geographic areas
$ Given: A few grants are awarded annually; $22,000 - $25,000 stipend for 2 years of predoctoral research, $30,000 - $35,000 stipend for 2 years of postdoctoral research, plus travel and research allowance
Application Information: Write for details
Deadline: October 15
Contact: Christopher Hale, Fellowship Coordinator

. . . .

Harvard University
European Society and
Western Security
Research Fellowships *
Center for
International Affairs
1737 Cambridge Street
Cambridge, MA 02138
(617) 495-9899

Description: Fellowships for doctoral candidates at dissertation level and postdoctoral scholars in European studies, international relations, and arms control; tenable at Harvard's Center for International Affairs and Center for European Affairs for study of the relationship between European society and Western security; recipients chosen on the basis of academic achievement and proposed research
Restrictions: Preference to U.S. citizens
$ Given: 6 fellowships awarded annually; $12,000 predoctoral stipend, $24,000 postdoctoral stipend, plus medical insurance contribution
Application Information: Write for details
Deadline: February 19
Contact: Jean Shildneck, Fellowships Coordinator

Harvard University
Harvard International
Institutions Fellowships *
Center for
International Affairs
1737 Cambridge Street
Cambridge, MA 02138
(617) 495-9899

Description: Residential fellowships at Harvard's Center for International Affairs for doctoral candidates and recent PhDs conducting research on international institutions; one-year fellowship includes participation in seminar/conference program; recipients chosen on the basis of academic achievement and proposed research
Restrictions: N/A
$ Given: 4-6 fellowships awarded annually; $14,000 predoctoral stipend, $24,000 postdoctoral stipend, plus health insurance and university fees
Application Information: Write for details
Deadline: February 7
Contact: Jean Shildneck, Fellowships Coordinator

Lesley College
Cambridge Partnership
Award
29 Everett Street
Cambridge, MA 02138
(617) 868-9600

Description: Scholarship grants for female undergraduates
Restrictions: Must be a Cambridge resident who graduated from Cambridge Rindge and Latin High School. Must demonstrate academic achievement and leadership.
$ Given: 2 grants of $2,500 each
Application Information: Write for guidelines.
Deadline: May 1
Contact: F. Duane Quinn, Director of Financial Aid

• •

Lesley College
Middle School
Mathematics/Science
Teacher Award
29 Everett Street
Cambridge, MA 02138
(617) 868-9600

Description: Scholarship grants for undergraduates
Restrictions: Must major in middle school education and specialize in mathematics or science. Selection is based on high school achievement and SAT score. Must also demonstrate an interest in science and math through high school activities.
$ Given: 14 grants of $1,000 each
Application Information: Write for guidelines.
Deadline: April 1
Contact: Linda Schulman, Associate Professor, Middle School Math/Science

Massachusetts
Institute of Technology
Charles J. Paine
Scholarship Fund Trust
c/o Taylor, Granson & Perrin
160 Franklin St.
Boston, MA 02110
(617) 951-2777

Description: Scholarship grants
Restrictions: N/A
$ Given: 6 grants of $1,500-$3,500
Application Information: Must submit an initial letter describing financial need and biographical information.
Deadline: N/A
Contact: Charles M. Granson, Jr., Trustee

Massachusetts
Institute of Technology
Gorman Foundation
c/o Wayne L. Millsap, P.C.
7777 Bonhomme St.
Suite 2300
Clayton, MO 063105
(314) 726-6545

Description: Scholarship grants
Restrictions: The applicant must be a resident of St. Louis who graduated from a St. Louis high school.
$ Given: 25 grants ranging from $1,250-$3,000
Application Information: Write for guidelines.
Deadline: November 1 for the semester starting in January and May 31 for the semester starting June and August
Contact: N/A

• • • • • • • • • • • • • • • • • • •

Stonehill College
Anthony E. Cascino
Scholarship
320 Washington St.
North Easton, MA 02357
(508) 230-1347

Description: Scholarship grants for juniors and seniors
Restrictions: Student must study marketing.
$ Given: 4 grants of $1,000-$2,000 each
Application Information: Write for guidelines.
Deadline: April 15
Contact: Eileen K. O'Leary, Director of Student Aid and Finance

Stonehill College
Edmond M. Moriarty, Jr.
Scholarship
320 Washington St.
North Easton, MA 02357
(508) 230-1347

Description: Scholarship grants for undergraduates studying business administration; there are two awards for Business Administration majors and two awards for children of employees of the New York or American Stock Exchange. The latter are renewable.
Restrictions: See above.
$ Given: 4 grants of $2,900-$9,400 each
Application Information: Write for guidelines.
Deadline: April 15, February 15 for incoming freshmen
Contact: Eileen K. O'Leary, Director of Student Aid and Finance

Stonehill College
Stephen P. Mandill
Memorial Scholarship
320 Washington St.
North Easton, MA 02357
(508) 230-1347

Description: Scholarship grants for Massachusetts residents
Restrictions: Must be a sophomore, junior, or senior in Business Administration.
$ Given: 5 grants of $1,000 each
Application Information: Write for guidelines.
Deadline: April 15
Contact: Eileen K. O'Leary, Director of Student Aid and Finance

• • • • • • • • • • • • • • • • • • • •

Tufts University
Philip V. Fava and Nancy
Owen Fava Scholarship
Tufts University
Medical College
Medford, MA 02155
(508) 381-3395

Description: Scholarship grants
Restrictions: N/A
$ Given: 10 grants of $350-$600
Application Information: Write for guidelines.
Deadline: October
Contact: Robert H. Fava, Executive Trustee

University of Massachusetts
Centennial Educational
Trust Fund *
Shawmut Bank of
Hampshire County
Amherst, MA 01022
(413) 256-5511

Description: Scholarship grants for seniors
Restrictions: See above.
$ Given: 6 grants of $3,000 each
Application Information: Write for guidelines.
Deadline: June 1
Contact: Robert J. Coleman

Williams College
Gaius Charles Bolin
Fellowships for Minority
Graduate Students *
Hopkins Hall
Williamstown, MA 02167

Description: Scholarship grants for minority predoctoral candidates in the humanities or in the natural, social, or behavioral sciences to work towards the completion of dissertation work
Restrictions: Must be a U.S. citizen and have completed doctoral work except the dissertation.
$ Given: 2 grants of $22,000 plus a maximum of $2,000 research expenses allowance
Application Information: Submit a full curriculum vitae, a graduate school transcript and 3 letters of recommendation, a copy of dissertation prospectus, and a description of teaching interests.
Deadline: February 28
Contact: John Reichert, Dean of the Faculty

MICHIGAN

Hope College
Distinguished Artist Award
Office of Admissions
Holland, MI 49423-3698
(616) 394-7850

Description: Scholarship grants for freshmen and transfers
Restrictions: Must plan to study one of the fine arts (art, dance, music, theatre) and have a minimum 2.5 GPA.
$ Given: 20 grants of $1,300 each
Application Information: Write for guidelines.
Deadline: March 1
Contact: Department chairperson

Madonna College
Deseranno Educational
Foundation, Inc.
c/o The Right Reverend
Ferdinand DeCheudt
Father Taillieu Senior
Citizen Home, Inc.
18760 East Thirteenth Mile Rd.
Roseville, MI 48060

Description: Scholarship grants for undergraduates
Restrictions: See above
$ Given: 16 grants of $850-$3,000 each
Application Information: Write for guidelines.
Deadline: N/A
Contact: Ferdinand De Cheudt

Northern
Michigan University
Edgar L. Harden
Academic Scholarship
Marquette, MI 49855
(906) 227-2327

Description: Scholarship grants for freshmen
Restrictions: Must qualify through an on-campus competition.
$ Given: 6 grants of $4,000 each
Application Information: Scholarship competition is held in October of every year. Write for guidelines.
Deadline: November 15
Contact: Robert L. Pecotte, Director of Financial Aid

• •

Northern Michigan University Presidential Scholarship
Marquette, MI 49855
(906) 227-2327

Description: Scholarship grants for Michigan residents
Restrictions: Must rank in the upper fifth of class and have a minimum 3.5 GPA.
$ Given: 4 grants of $4,000 each
Application Information: An on-campus competition is the basis for selections. Write for guidelines.
Deadline: N/A
Contact: N/A

University of Detroit BSAF Wyandotte Scholarship
4001 West McNichols Road
Detroit, MI 48221
(313) 927-1000

Description: Scholarship grants
Restrictions: N/A
$ Given: $41,000
Application Information: Applicants are interviewed by a member of the faculty and a representative of BSAF Wyandotte Corporation. Write for guidelines.
Deadline: N/A
Contact: N/A

University of Detroit Chemistry Department Scholarship
4001 West McNichols Rd.
Detroit, MI 48221
(313) 927-1000

Description: Scholarship grants for chemistry majors
Restrictions: See above.
$ Given: 4 grants of $1,000 each
Application Information: Write for guidelines.
Deadline: N/A
Contact: N/A

University of Detroit Jesuit Founders Transfer Student Scholarship
4001 West McNichols Road
Detroit, MI 48221
(313) 927-1000

Description: Scholarship grants for sophomore transfer students
Restrictions: Must be a transfer student from a community college with a minimum 3.5 GPA and have an associate's degree.
$ Given: 54 grants ranging from $2,250-$4,080.
Application Information: Write for guidelines.
Deadline: March 15
Contact: Office of Admissions

. . . .

University of Detroit
St. Louis Alumni
Engineering Scholarship
4001 West McNichols Rd.
Detroit, MI 48221
(313) 927-1000

Description: Scholarship grant for engineering students
Restrictions: Must be from the St. Louis area.
$ Given: $5,400
Application Information: Write for guidelines.
Deadline: N/A
Contact: N/A

University of
Michigan at Ann Arbor
Academic Recognition
Scholarship
Office of Financial Aid
2011 SAB
Ann Arbor, MI 48109-1316
(313) 763-4149

Description: Scholarship grants for freshmen in Art, Education, Music, Natural Resources, and Nursing
Restrictions: Must be an out-of-state resident.
$ Given: 15 grants of $2,000 each
Application Information: No application is necessary. Recipients are selected by GPA and test scores on their admissions applications.
Deadline: N/A
Contact: N/A

University of
Michigan at Ann Arbor
Backham Undergraduate
Scholarship
Office of Financial Aid
2011 SAB
Ann Arbor, MI 48109-1316
(313) 763-4119

Description: Scholarship grants for freshmen
Restrictions: Must be honors students from Michigan.
$ Given: 4 grants of $1,000 each
Application Information: No need to apply. Honors students are identified and invited to apply.
Deadline: February 10
Contact: Vivian Byrd, Editor

University of
Michigan at Ann Arbor
Bentley Scholarship
Office of Financial Aid
2011 SAB
Ann Arbor, MI 48109-1316
(313) 763-4119

Description: Scholarship grants for freshmen
Restrictions: Must be a Michigan resident with a high GPA and test scores.
$ Given: 2 grants of $8,119 each
Application Information: No application required. Candidates are selected on the basis of the restrictions listed above and an interview.
Deadline: N/A
Contact: Vivian Byrd, Editor

MICHIGAN

• •

University of Michigan at Ann Arbor Regents Alumni Scholarship
Office of Financial Aid
2011 SAB
Ann Arbor, MI 48109-1316
(313) 763-4119

Description: Scholarship grants for freshmen
Restrictions: Must be a Michigan resident with a high GPA and high test scores.
$ Given: 345 grants of $1,000 each
Application Information: Write for guidelines.
Deadline: February 1
Contact: Vivian Byrd, Editor

Western Michigan University Higher Education Incentive Scholarship
Kalamazoo, MI 49008
(616) 387-6000

Description: Scholarship grants for freshmen in the earth sciences
Restrictions: Must be a minority student with a minimum 3.5 high school GPA.
$ Given: 10 grants of $4,000 each
Application Information: Write for guidelines.
Deadline: January 10
Contact: Robert M. Zellers, Assistant Director of Financial Aid

Western Michigan University Phi Theta Kappa Alumni Scholarship
Kalamazoo, MI 49008
(616) 387-6000

Description: Scholarship grants for transfer students from community colleges
Restrictions: Must be a member of a Phi Theta Kappa chapter with an Associate's degree and a minimum 3.5 GPA for transferable course work. Must also have a recommendation from the chapter advisor.
$ Given: 14 grants of $1,000 each
Application Information: Write for guidelines.
Deadline: March 15
Contact: Robert M. Zellers, Assistant Director of Financial Aid

MINNESOTA

Bethel College
Music Scholarship
3900 Bethel Drive
Saint Paul, MN 55112-6999
(612) 638-6241

Description: Scholarship grants for freshmen
Restrictions: See above.
$ Given: 6 grants of $1,000 each
Application Information: Write for guidelines.
Deadline: March 1
Contact: Daniel C. Nelson, Director of College
Financial Planning

Northwestern College
Leadership Award
3303 North Snelling Avenue
Saint Paul, MN 55113
(612) 631-5100

Description: Scholarship grants for freshmen
Restrictions: Must be a non-Minnesota resident and
demonstrate leadership potential.
$ Given: 92 grants of $1,000 each
Application Information: Write for guidelines.
Deadline: Rolling
Contact: Ralph Anderson, Dean of Admissions

University of Minnesota
Adelle and Erwin
Tomash Fellowships in the
History of Information *
Charles Babbage Institute,
University of Minnesota
103 Walter Library
117 Pleasant St., SE
Minneapolis, MN 55455
(612) 624-5050

Description: Scholarship grant for graduate students
Restrictions: Must be studying for a PhD in Information
Processing.
$ Given: $8,500
Application Information: Submit biographical data;
research plan containing a statement and justification of a
research problem, and evidence of faculty support for the
project; three letters of reference, certified transcripts of
college credits and GRE scores. There is no application form.
Priority will be given to those who have completed all
requirements for a doctoral degree except research and
writing of a dissertation. Fellows may reapply for up to 2 one
year continuations of the Fellowship.
Deadline: January 15
Contact: Judy A. Cilcain, Associate Administrator

• •

**University of Minnesota
Agricultural Merit
Scholarships**
260 Williamson Hall
231 Pillsbury Drive, SE
Minneapolis, MN 55455
(612) 373-5000

Description: Scholarship grants for freshmen
Restrictions: Must major in Agriculture, either rank in the top ten percentile of his/her high school class or be a transfer student with a minimum 3.5 GPA. Leadership ability and interest in agriculture is also considered.
$ Given: Fifty grants of $1,000-$3,000
Application Information: Write for guidelines.
Deadline: N/A
Contact: Keith Wharton

**University of Minnesota
Dayton Kirkham
Scholarship**
260 Williamson Hall
231 Pillsbury Drive, SE
Minneapolis, MN 55455
(612) 373-5000

Description: Scholarship grants
Restrictions: The grant is based on high school rank, test scores, and the applicant's interest in natural resource management.
$ Given: 7 grants of $1,000 each
Application Information: Write for guidelines.
Deadline: N/A
Contact: John V. Bell

**University of Minnesota
Undergraduate Assistant
Scholarship**
260 Williamson Hall
231 Pillsbury Drive, SE
Minneapolis, MN 55455
(612) 373-5000

Description: Scholarship grants for science majors
Restrictions: Selection is based on high school rank, test scores, math and science grades 9-12, and an essay.
$ Given: 25 grants of $1,000 each.
Application Information: Write for guidelines.
Deadline: N/A
Contact: Gail Fraser

**University of
Minnesota at Duluth
Edwin H. Eddy Family
Foundation ***
c/o Norwest Bank Duluth, N.A.
Capital Management and
Trust Department
Duluth, MN 55802

Description: Scholarship grants for Duluth, Minnesota area residents.
Restrictions: Must be graduate or undergraduate students in the field of communication disorders with a minimum 3.0 GPA.
$ Given: Grants of $1,200 each
Application Information: Write for guidelines.
Deadline: March 31
Contact: Murray George, Trustee

**University of
Minnesota at Morris
Presidential Scholarship**
Admissions and Financial Aid
Morris, MN 56267
(612) 589-6035

Description: Scholarship grants for freshmen
Restrictions: Must be a Minnesota resident and rank in the top twentieth of graduating class.
$ Given: 45 grants of $1,000 each
Application Information: Must submit an application and an essay. Write for guidelines.
Deadline: February 1
Contact: Robert Vidanker, Director of Financial Aid and Admissions

MISSISSIPPI

**Rust College
Academic Dean's
Scholarship**
150 Rust Avenue
Holly Springs, MS 38635
(601) 252-4661

Description: Scholarship grants for freshmen
Restrictions: Must rank in top tenth of high school graduating class, have a minimum 3.0 GPA, and have a minimum ACT score of 18.
$ Given: 15 grants of $1,500
Application Information: Write for guidelines.
Deadline: N/A
Contact: Helen L. Street, Director of Student Financial Aid

MISSISSIPPI

. . . .

**University of Mississippi
Hearin-Hess Scholarship
in Business**
University, MS 38677
(601) 232-7175

Description: Scholarship grants for freshmen who intend to major in business
Restrictions: Must hold superior high school academic record, strong ACT score, and leadership ability.
$ Given: 10 grants of $3,000 each
Application Information: Write for guidelines.
Deadline: April 1
Contact: Betty U. Magee, Scholarship Coordinator

**University of Mississippi
Regional Scholarship**
University, MS 38677
(601) 232-7175

Description: Scholarship grants for undergraduates
Restrictions: Must be a non-Mississippi resident with a minimum ACT score of 21 and rank in top third of class.
$ Given: 60 grants of $1,462
Application Information: Write for guidelines.
Deadline: April 1
Contact: Betty Magee, Scholarship Coordinator

**University of
Southern Mississippi
Art and Art Education
Graduate Assistantship ***
P.O. Box 5033
Southern Station
Hattiesburg, MS 39406
(601) 266-4972

Description: Scholarship grants in the form of teaching assistantships primarily for students with a BFA or BA in art, who seek graduate study in art education.
Restrictions: See above.
$ Given: $5,500
Application Information: Write for guidelines.
Deadline: N/A
Contact: Jerry Walden, Chair, Department of Art

MISSOURI

St. Louis University
Rosalie Tilles Nonsectarian
Charity Fund Scholarship
705 Olive Street
Suite 906
St. Louis, MO 63101
(314) 231-1721

Description: Scholarship grants for graduating high school seniors who reside in Missouri.
Restrictions: Must be in top tenth of class and have a minimum 3.0 GPA.
$ Given: 12 grants of $2,500 each
Application Information: Write for guidelines.
Deadline: March 30
Contact: Rosalie Tilles Nonsectarian Charity Fund

Southwest Missouri
State University
Council on Public Higher
Education Scholarship
901 South National
Springfield, MO 65804
(417) 836-5262

Description: Scholarship grants for undergraduates in Education
Restrictions: Must be preparing for careers as mathematics, biology, chemistry, physics, or foreign language teachers at the elementary and secondary levels and must have completed a minimum of 75 hours.
$ Given: 10 grants of $1,000 each
Application Information: Write for guidelines.
Deadline: May 18
Contact: Brad Fuller, Scholarship Coordinator

Southwest Missouri
State University
Emily Nelson Moseley
Memorial Scholarship *
901 South National
Springfield, MO 65804
(417) 836-5262

Description: Scholarship grants for juniors, seniors and graduate students in Special Education.
Restrictions: Selection is based on academic performance, and recipients must enroll in the Reading and Special Education Department.
$ Given: 3 grants of $2,000 each
Application Information: Write for guidelines.
Deadline: May 1
Contact: Brad Fuller, Scholarship Coordinator

. . . .

Southwest Missouri State University Florence C. Painter Memorial Scholarship *
901 South National
Springfield, MO 65804
(417) 836-5262

Description: Scholarship grants for seniors and graduate students in Secondary Education
Restrictions: Must have a minimum 3.0 GPA and must show financial need. Preference is given to those planning to teach Spanish.
$ Given: 2 grants of $2,000 each
Application Information: Write for guidelines.
Deadline: May 1
Contact: Brad Fuller, Scholarship Coordinator

Southwest Missouri State University Foreign Languages Regents Scholarship
901 South National
Springfield, MO 65804
(417) 836-5262

Description: Scholarship grants for undergraduates majoring in foreign languages
Restrictions: Must have a minimum 3.0 GPA and at least 12 hours of one language with an "A" in each course, must agree to take 2 upper-level foreign language courses, one of which must be taken while on the scholarship, and recipients must participate in departmental events.
$ Given: 4 grants of $1,000-$1,200 each
Application Information: Write for guidelines.
Deadline: N/A
Contact: Brad Fuller, Scholarship Coordinator

Southwest Missouri State University Inmon Memorial Scholarship *
901 South National
Springfield, MO 65804
(417) 836-5262

Description: Scholarship grants for seniors and graduate students of Business.
Restrictions: Must be a U.S. citizen and must carry 12 hours or more each semester with a minimum 3.2 GPA. Preference is given to native Missourians.
$ Given: Ten grants of $1,962-$3,786
Application Information: Write for guidelines.
Deadline: February 8
Contact: Brad Fuller, Scholarship Coordinator

• •

Southwest Missouri
State University
In-School Players
Scholarship
901 South National
Springfield, MO 65804
(417) 836-5262

Description: Scholarship grants for undergraduates in Theatre or Dance
Restrictions: Must have performance experience in acting and/or music.
$ Given: 6 grants of $1,000-$1,200
Application Information: Write for guidelines.
Deadline: N/A
Contact: Brad Fuller, Scholarship Coordinator

Southwest Missouri
State University
Junior and Community
College President's
Scholarship
901 South National
Springfield, MO 65804
(417) 836-5262

Description: Scholarship grants for undergraduates
Restrictions: Must be nominated by Presidents of Missouri Public Junior and Community Colleges, and recipients must have at least 30 credit hours.
$ Given: 32 grants ranging from $2,326-$4,186.
Application Information: Write for guidelines.
Deadline: N/A
Contact: Brad Fuller, Scholarship Coordinator

Southwest Missouri
State University
Junior and Community
College Regents
Scholarship
901 South National
Springfield, MO 65804
(417) 836-5262

Description: Scholarship grants for Missouri residents
Restrictions: Must have an Associate Degree or 60 hours of acceptable credit from a Missouri Junior or Community College with a minimum 3.4 GPA.
$ Given: 16 grants ranging from $1,000-$1,200
Application Information: Write for guidelines.
Deadline: May 1
Contact: Brad Fuller, Scholarship Coordinator

•   •   •   •   •   •   •   •   •   •   •   •   •   •   •   •   •   •   •   •

Southwest Missouri
State University
Music Regents Scholarship
901 South National
Springfield, MO 65804
(417) 836-5262

Description: Scholarship grants for undergraduates in Music
Restrictions: The recipients must maintain a minimum 2.5 GPA, with a 2.75 GPA in Music and continue to show promise of success in performance.
$ Given: 16 grants of $1,000-$1,200
Application Information: The recipients are selected by audition.
Deadline: N/A
Contact: Brad Fuller, Scholarship Coordinator

Southwest Missouri
State University
Theatre and Dance Activity
Regents Scholarship
901 South National
Springfield, MO 65804
(417) 836-5262

Description: Scholarship grants for undergraduates in Theatre and Dance
Restrictions: Recipients must maintain a minimum 2.5 GPA, participate in related activities, submit a departmental faculty recommendation, and reapply for renewal.
$ Given: 16 grants of $1,000-$1,200
Application Information: An audition or technical interview is required. Write for additional guidelines.
Deadline: February 20
Contact: Brad Fuller, Scholarship Coordinator.

Southwest Missouri
State University
Undergraduate Work Grant
901 South National
Springfield, MO 65804
(417) 836-5262

Description: Scholarship grants for undergraduates studying physics and astronomy
Restrictions: Must demonstrate academic achievement and interest in science.
$ Given: 4 grants of $1,000 each
Application Information: Write for guidelines.
Deadline: N/A
Contact: Brad Fuller, Scholarship Coordinator

• • • • • • • • • • • • • • • • • • •

**University of
Missouri at Columbia
The Marvin Boyer Memorial
Scholarship Fund**
382 Hawthorne St.
Patosi, MO 63664
(314) 438-2534

Description: Scholarship grants for undergraduates.
Restrictions: See above.
$ Given: N/A
Application Information: Write for guidelines.
Deadline: February 1
Contact: Shelly Miller

**University of
Missouri at Columbia
Mildred L. Ayres Trust**
c/o First National Bank of
Kansas City
14 West Tenth St.
Kansas City, MO 64183
or APPLICATION ADDRESS:
P.O. Box 419038
Kansas City, MO 64105
(816) 221-2800

Description: Scholarship grants to assist with theological and medical training and living expenses
Restrictions: Must be a resident of Missouri. Preference is given to residents of metropolitan Kansas City.
$ Given: 5 grants of $750-$1,500
Application Information: Write for guidelines.
Deadline: N/A
Contact: David P. Ross

**University of
Missouri at Columbia
Rosalie Tilles Nonsectarian
Charity Fund Scholarship**
705 Olive Street
Suite 906
St. Louis, MO 63101
(314) 231-1721

Description: Scholarship grants for graduating high school seniors planning to attend the University of Missouri at Columbia.
Restrictions: Must be a resident of Missouri and be in top tenth of class.
$ Given: 12 grants of $2,500 each
Application Information: Write for guidelines.
Deadline: March 30
Contact: Rosalie Tilles Nonsectarian Charity Fund

**University of
Missouri at Kansas City
Victor E. Speas Foundation**
c/o Boatmen's First National
Bank of Kansas City
14 West Tenth St.
Kansas City, MO 64183
(816) 691-7481

Description: Scholarship grants for medical students
Restrictions: See above.
$ Given: Unspecified number of grants totalling $1,262,212
Application Information: Write for guidelines.
Deadline: N/A
Contact: David P. Ross, Senior Vice-President

• • • • • • • • • • • • • • • • • • • •

**University of
Missouri at Rolla
Gorman Foundation**
c/o Wayne L. Millsap, P.C.
7777 Bonhomme St.
Suite 2300
Clayton, MO 063105
(314) 726-6545

Description: Scholarship grants for St. Louis residents
Restrictions: Must have graduated from a St. Louis
high school.
$ Given: 25 grants of $1,250-$3,000
Application Information: Write for guidelines.
Deadline: November 1 for the semester starting in January
and May 31 for the semester starting June and August
Contact: N/A

**University of
Missouri at Rolla
The Marvin Boyer Memorial
Scholarship Fund**
382 Hawthorne St.
Patosi, MO 63664
(314) 438-2534

Description: Scholarship grants for undergraduates.
Restrictions: See above.
$ Given: N/A
Application Information: Write for guidelines.
Deadline: February 1
Contact: Shelly Miller

**University of
Missouri at Rolla
Minority Engineering
Program Scholarship**
204 Rolla Building
Rolla, MO 65401
(314) 341-4212

Description: Scholarship grants for freshmen.
Restrictions: Must attend a 7-week summer program at the
University of Missouri—Rolla prior to Fall enrollment.
$ Given: 10 grants of $5,500 each.
Application Information: Write for guidelines.
Deadline: December 31
Contact: Floyd Harris, Director, Minority Engineering
Program

**Washington University
Chancellor's Graduate
Fellowships for African
Americans ***
Campus Box 1187
1 Brookings Drive
St. Louis, MO 63130-4899
(314) 889-6821

Description: Scholarship grant for African-American
graduate students in any Phd or DSc programs in arts and
science, business, engineering, or social work
Restrictions: Must be interested in becoming college or
university professors.
$ Given: $15,000 per year plus full tuition scholarship
Application Information: Write for guidelines.
Deadline: January 15
Contact: Joyce A. Edwards, Coordinator, Graduate Student
Affairs and Services

• • • • • • • • • • • • • • • • • • •

**Washington University
May and Wallace Cady
Memorial Trust**
c/o Commerce Bank of
St. Louis, N.A.
8000 Forsyth Boulevard
Clayton, MO 63105
(314) 726-3600

Description: Scholarship grant
Restrictions: Must be a graduate of United Presbyterian
Homes of Synod, Texas.
$ Given: $4,100
Application Information: Write for guidelines.
Deadline: N/A
Contact: Gerald L. Wedemeier, Assistant Vice-President

**Washington University
Rosalie Tilles Nonsectarian
Charity Fund Scholarship**
705 Olive Street
Suite 906
St. Louis, MO 63101
(314) 231-1721

Description: Scholarship grants for graduating high school
seniors planning to attend Washington University.
Restrictions: Must be a Missouri resident, be in top tenth of
class, and have a minimum 3.0 GPA.
$ Given: 12 grants of $2,500 each
Application Information: Write for guidelines.
Deadline: March 30
Contact: Rosalie Tilles Nonsectarian Charity Fund

**William Jewell College
Frank H. Davidson Trust**
Allen Bank and Trust
Company
100 East Pearl
Harrisonville, MO 64701-1846

Description: Scholarship grants for graduating high
school seniors
Restrictions: Must be from Harrisonville, Missouri,
high school.
$ Given: Grants totalling $6,000
Application Information: Write for guidelines.
Deadline: N/A
Contact: Dayle P. Lindsey

**William Jewell College
Mildred L. Ayres Trust**
c/o First National Bank
of Kansas City
14 West Tenth St.
P.O. Box 409138
Kansas City, MO 64105
(816) 234-7481

Description: Scholarship grants to assist with theological
and medical training and living expenses
Restrictions: The applicant must be a resident of Missouri.
Preference is given to residents of metropolitan Kansas City.
$ Given: 5 grants of $750-$1,500.
Application Information: Write for guidelines.
Deadline: N/A
Contact: David P. Ross

MISSOURI

• • • • • • • • • • • • • • • • • • • •

William Woods College Equestrian Science Department Scholarship
William Woods College
200 West 12th
Fulton, MO 65251
(314) 642-2251

Description: Scholarship grant for a freshman specializing in Equestrian Science
Restrictions: Must demonstrate academic achievement and riding skills at a quality level.
$ Given: 25 grants of $1,000 each
Application Information: Write for guidelines.
Deadline: May 11
Contact: Laura Archuleta, Director for Financial Aid

MONTANA

University of Montana George E. Bright Memorial Fellowship
Financial Aid Office
Missoula, MT 59812
(406) 243-5373

Description: Scholarship grants for students in the field of natural resource management
Restrictions: The applicant must major in natural resource management and have excellent academic credentials and recommendations.
$ Given: 3-4 grants of $2,000 each
Application Information: Write for guidelines.
Deadline: February 15
Contact: Nancy DeVerse

University of Montana Harry S. Truman Scholarship
Financial Aid Office
Missoula, MT 59812
(406) 243-5373

Description: Scholarship grants for undergraduates majoring in a field that will lead to a career in public service
Restrictions: Must have a superior academic record, interest in public service, and must demonstrate a commitment to future governmental service.
$ Given: 39 grants of $7,000 each
Application Information: Write for guidelines.
Deadline: October 20
Contact: Dr. James Lopach, Political Science Department

• • • • • • • • • • • • • • • • • • • •

University of Montana
Paul Douglas Teacher
Scholarship
Montana Commission on
Higher Education
33 South Last Chance Gulch
Helena, MT 59620
(406) 444-6594

Description: Scholarship grants for undergraduates in
Education
Restrictions: Must be a U.S. citizen, reside in Montana, and
rank in the top tenth of their high school classes. Recipients
of the award must attend a program leading to the teaching
profession in grades K-12.
$ Given: 5-10 grants of $5,000 each
Application Information: Write for guidelines.
Deadline: N/A
Contact: Bill Lannan

Western Montana College
Mary Baker Emerick Art
Scholarship
710 South Atlantic
Dillon, MT 59725
(406) 683-7511

Description: Scholarship grants for undergraduates
Restrictions: Must have talent and ability in art. Recipients
must submit a competitive portfolio and meet departmental
standards each year for renewal.
$ Given: 30 grants of a minimum of $1,000 each
Application Information: Applicants must submit a
completed application and submit a portfolio.
Deadline: March 1
Contact: Michele O'Neill, Director of Admission

William Woods College
Christian Church Grant
200 West 12th
Fulton, MO 65251
(314) 642-2251

Description: Scholarship grants for undergraduates
Restrictions: Must be an active member in the Disciples of
Christ Church.
$ Given: 10 grants of $1,000 each
Application Information: Write for guidelines.
Deadline: August 1
Contact: Laura Archuleta, Director for Financial Aid

NEBRASKA

**Bellevue College
Business Divisional
Scholarship**
Financial Aid Office
Galvin Road at Harvell Drive
Bellevue, NE 68005
(402) 293-3762

Description: Scholarship grants for undergraduates
Restrictions: Must have a minimum 3.0 GPA and full-time status.
$ Given: Five grants of $1,095 each
Application Information: Write for guidelines.
Deadline: June 1
Contact: Linda M. Barrows

**Bellevue College
Professional Studies
Ambassador Scholarship**
Financial Aid Office
Galvin Road at Harvell Drive
Bellevue, NE 68005
(402) 293-3762

Description: Scholarship grants for juniors and seniors majoring in Management of Human Resources
Restrictions: Must demonstrate professionalism at work and a history of positive influence on others through community service and political involvement.
$ Given: 8 grants of $1,000 each
Application Information: Write for guidelines.
Deadline: May 15
Contact: Linda M. Barrow, Director of Financial Aid

**Bellevue College
Professional Studies
Merit Award**
Financial Aid Office
Galvin Road at Harvell Drive
Bellevue, NE 68005
(402) 293-3762

Description: Scholarship grants for juniors and seniors
Restrictions: Must be studying Management of Human Resources and have financial needs.
$ Given: 4 grants of $1,000 each
Application Information: Write for guidelines.
Deadline: May 15
Contact: Linda M. Barrow, Director of Financial Aid

Chadron State College Board of Trustees Scholarship
10th and Main Streets
Chadron, NE 69337-2690
(308) 432-6230

Description: Scholarship grants for freshmen
Restrictions: Must be a Nebraska resident. Must have a minimum ACT score of 25 and rank in top quarter of high school graduating class.
$ Given: 80 grants of $1,296 each
Application Information: Write for guidelines.
Deadline: January 15
Contact: Del Hussey, Director of Financial Aid

Creighton University Luce Scholarship
2500 California St.
Omaha, NE 68178
(402) 280-2731

Description: Scholarship grants for female juniors studying science
Restrictions: Must desire a career in scientific research and possess strong academic skills in math and science.
$ Given: 5 grants ranging from $4,653-$11,369
Application Information: Write for guidelines.
Deadline: March 1
Contact: Robert Human, Assistant Director of Financial Aid

Kearney State College Board of Trustees Scholarship
905 West 25th
Kearney, NE 68849
(308) 234-8520

Description: Scholarship grants for freshmen
Restrictions: Must be a resident of Nebraska, rank in top quarter of high school graduating class, and have a minimum ACT score of 24.
$ Given: 50 grants of $1,232 each
Application Information: Write for guidelines.
Deadline: January 15, March 15
Contact: Varlene Jacoby, Financial Aid Counselor

University of Nebraska at Lincoln Regents Scholarship
Office of Scholarships and Financial Aid
14th and "R" Streets
Lincoln, NE 68588-0411
(402) 472-2030

Description: Scholarship grants for freshmen
Restrictions: Must be a Nebraska high school graduate with strong academic credentials.
$ Given: 350 grants of $1,900-$2,100 each
Application Information: Write for guidelines.
Deadline: December 15
Contact: John E. Beacon, Director of Admissions, Scholarships and Financial Aid

• • • • • • • • • • • • • • • • • •

NEVADA

Sierra Nevada College
Drown Scholarship
P.O. Box 4269
800 College Drive
Incline Village, NV 89450

Description: Scholarship grants for undergraduates
Restrictions: Must be a Business major with a minimum 3.5 GPA.
$ Given: 7 grants of $2,500 each
Application Information: Write for guidelines.
Deadline: June 1
Contact: Brad Beckwith, Director of Admissions

University of Nevada
at Las Vegas
Louis A. Woitishek
Educational Fund
c/o First Interstate
Bank of Nevada
Trust Dept.
P.O. Box 98588
Las Vegas, NV 89193-8588
(702) 791-6139

Description: Scholarship grants for residents of Clark County, NV
Restrictions: See above
$ Given: 19 grants of $550-$1,100 each
Application Information: Write for guidelines.
Deadline: March 15
Contact: N/A

NEW HAMPSHIRE

Dartmouth College
Wheelock, Vermont,
Scholarship
McNutt Hall
Second Floor
Hanover, NH 03755
(603) 646-2453

Description: Scholarship grants for undergraduates
Restrictions: Must have been born in Wheelock, VT, or be a resident of the town with financial needs, and must remain in Wheelock to maintain eligibility.
$ Given: 15 grants up to $16,230 each
Application Information: Write for guidelines.
Deadline: February 15
Contact: Virginia S. Hazen, Director of Financial Aid

• •

Dartmouth College Humanities Research Institute Resident Research Fellowships
307 Wentworth Hall
Hanover, NH 03755
(603) 646-3756

Description: Residential fellowships at Dartmouth College for doctoral candidates at dissertation level and recent PhDs in the humanities and social sciences; provides access to resources and includes participation in a 10-week research institute; recipients chosen on the basis of proposed research
Restrictions: Doctoral candidates must have completed all requirements other than dissertation
$ Given: An unspecified number of fellowships awarded annually; each with $3500 stipend, plus office space and use of library
Application Information: Write for details
Deadline: Varies
Contact: Sandra Gregg, Assistant Dean

NEW JERSEY

College of Saint Elizabeth Genevieve A. Walsh Scholarship
Convent Station, NJ 07961
(201) 292-6300

Description: Scholarship grants for freshmen
Restrictions: Must be a women with a visual, mobility, or auditory impairment due to a physical disability.
$ Given: 2 grants ranging from $3,000-$7,500.
Application Information: Write for guidelines.
Deadline: June 1
Contact: Sister Ann Michele Texido, Director of Financial Aid

Drew University Achievement Scholarship
Madison Ave.
Madison, NJ 07940
(201) 408-3253

Description: Scholarship grant for minority students
Restrictions: Must demonstrate financial need.
$ Given: $4,000
Application Information: Write for guidelines.
Deadline: N/A
Contact: James Diverio, Associate Director of College Admissions

. . . .

Drew University
Merit I Scholarship
Madison Ave.
Madison, NJ 07940
(201) 408-3253

Description: Scholarship grants for freshmen
Restrictions: Must rank in top 1% of class and have a minimum 1350 SAT.
$ Given: 74 grants of $12,000-$15,000 each
Application Information: Write for guidelines.
Deadline: January 1
Contact: James Diverio, Associate Director of College Admissions

Drew University
Merit II Scholarship
Madison Ave.
Madison, NJ 07940
(201) 408-3253

Description: Scholarship grants for freshmen
Restrictions: Must rank in top 5% of class and have a minimum 1350 SAT.
$ Given: 93 grants of $8,000-$11,000 each
Application Information: Write for guidelines.
Deadline: January 1
Contact: James Diverio, Associate Director of College Admissions

Drew University
Merit III Scholarship
Madison Ave.
Madison, NJ 07940
(201) 408-3253

Description: Scholarship grants for freshmen
Restrictions: Must rank in top 10% of class and have a minimum 1200 SAT.
$ Given: 26 grants of $4,000 each
Application Information: Write for guidelines.
Deadline: January 1
Contact: James Diverio, Associate Director of College Admissions.

New School for Music Study Graduate Fellowships in Piano Teaching *
P.O. Box 407
Princeton, NJ 08540
(609) 921-2900

Description: Scholarship grants for graduate students studying piano performance and teaching. The award is tenable at the New School for Music Study. An M.M. is offered in conjunction with Westminster Choir College.
Restrictions: Must demonstrate achievement and teaching potential and speak fluent English.
$ Given: 2-6 grants of $1,000-$5,000. Grant is renewable for up to 2 years.
Application Information: Write for guidelines.
Deadline: March 15
Contact: Sam Holland, Director

Princeton University Charles W. Caldwell Scholarship Fund *
c/o State Street Bank & Trust Company
P.O. Box 351
Boston, MA 02101

Description: Scholarship grants to male seniors
Restrictions: Must have plans for graduate study at Princeton.
$ Given: 2 grants of $3,000 each
Application Information: Write for guidelines.
Deadline: N/A
Contact: Sharon Doherty-Clancy

Princeton University Class of 1926 Foundation
Cardinal Rd.
Greenwich, CT 06830
(203) 869-2382

Description: Scholarship grant
Restrictions: See above.
$ Given: $5,000
Application Information: Write for guidelines.
Deadline: N/A
Contact: Gerald Hallock, Trustee

NEW JERSEY

• • • • • • • • • • • • • • • • • • • •

**Stevens Institute
of Technology
Academic Fellowship
(Merit Awards)**
Castle Point on the Hudson
Hoboken, NJ 07030
(201) 420-5194

Description: Scholarship grants for freshmen
Restrictions: Must hold superior record in test scores, GPA,
extracurricular activities, etc.
$ Given: 180 grants of $1,000-$5,000 each
Application Information: No formal application necessary.
Every freshman is automatically eligible.
Deadline: March 1
Contact: Peter A. Persuitti, Dean of Admissions and
Financial Aid

**Stockton State College
College Scholar**
Jimmy Leeds Road
Pomona, NJ 08240
(609) 652-1776

Description: Scholarship grants for freshmen
Restrictions: See above.
$ Given: 4 grants of $1,000 each
Application Information: Write for guidelines.
Deadline: N/A
Contact: John Rahmeyer, Interim Chief Development Officer

NEW MEXICO

**New Mexico Institute of
Mining and Technology
Counselor's Choice Award**
Financial Aid Office
Campus Station Box M
Socorro, NM 87801
(505) 835-5333

Description: Scholarship grant for freshmen
Restrictions: Must have a minimum high school GPA of 2.5,
have a minimum ACT score of 19 or the SAT equivalent, and
be recommended by a high school counselor (only one grant
per high school).
$ Given: 85 grants of $1,000 each
Application Information: Write for guidelines.
Deadline: March 1
Contact: Joe P. Martinez, Director, Student Financial Aid

• • • • • • • • • • • • • • • • • • • •

New Mexico Institute of Mining and Technology Regents Engineering Scholarship
Financial Aid Office
Campus Station Box M
Socorro, NM 87801
(505) 835-5333

Description: Scholarship grants for students studying engineering.
Restrictions: Preference is given to New Mexico residents.
$ Given: 50 grants of $1,000 each
Application Information: Write for guidelines.
Deadline: March 1
Contact: N/A

New Mexico State University Dollar Rent-a-Car Scholarship
P.O. Box 30001
Departments 5100
Las Cruces, NM 88003
(505) 646-4105

Description: Scholarship grants for undergraduates in Civil Engineering
Restrictions: Must demonstrate financial need and academic achievement.
$ Given: 4 grants of $1,000 each
Application Information: Write for guidelines.
Deadline: March 1
Contact: Dean of Engineering

New Mexico State University El Paso Natural Gas Company Scholarship
P.O. Box 30001
Departments 5100
Las Cruces, NM 88003
(505) 646-4105

Description: Scholarship grants for undergraduates
Restrictions: Must demonstrate scholastic ability and academic potential and study computer science with the management information system option, chemical or mechanical engineering accounting. Preference is given to a Spanish-American student.
$ Given: 4 grants of $1,000-$1,250
Application Information: Write for guidelines.
Deadline: March 1
Contact: N/A

University of Albuquerque Archbishop's Scholars Program
St. Joseph's Place, NW
Albuquerque, NM 87140
(505) 831-3333

Description: Scholarship grants for undergraduates
Restrictions: Must have cumulative "A" average in high school.
$ Given: 5 grants of $2,000 each
Application Information: Must submit 3 evaluation letters, including one from a high school counselor and one from a high school teacher. Must also submit an essay of approximately 500 words that describes personal highlights of high school education and future academic goals. Interviews are required.
Deadline: April 15
Contact: N/A

University of Albuquerque President's Scholars Program
St. Joseph's Place, NW
Albuquerque, NM 87140
(505) 831-3333

Description: Scholarship grants for freshmen entering in the spring semester and for freshmen transfer students (with less than 27 hours of college credit).
Restrictions: Must demonstrate achievement in academics and extracurricular activities.
$ Given: 10 grants of $1,000 each
Application Information: Must submit 3 evaluation letters, including one from a high school counselor and one from a high school teacher.
Deadline: April 15
Contact: N/A

University of Albuquerque Scholars Program
St. Joseph's Place, NW
Albuquerque, NM 87140
(505) 831-3333

Description: Scholarship grants for upperclassmen with a minimum 27 credit hours at the University of Albuquerque or elsewhere.
Restrictions: Must demonstrate achievement in academics and extracurricular activities and must have a minimum 3.5 GPA.
$ Given: 10 grants of $1,000 each
Application Information: Must submit a formal application and should also submit 3 evaluation letters from faculty members familiar with the candidate's academic work.
Deadline: April 15
Contact: N/A

• • • • • • • • • • • • • • • • • • •

University of New Mexico
New Mexico Scholars
University Hill
Financial Aid/
Scholarship Office
Albuquerque, NM 87131
(505) 277-2041

Description: Scholarship grants for freshmen
Restrictions: Must attend a New Mexico high school, have a minimum SAT combined score of 1020 or minimum ACT score of 25 and must demonstrate financial need.
$ Given: 218 grants of $1,953 each
Application Information: Write for guidelines.
Deadline: February 1
Contact: Roberta Lopez, Assistant Director of Financial Aid

NEW YORK

College of New Rochelle
College of New Rochelle
Scholarship
Castle Place
New Rochelle, NY 10805
(914) 654-5226

Description: Scholarship grants for the physically handicapped
Restrictions: See above.
$ Given: 10 grants of $1,000 each
Application Information: Write for guidelines.
Deadline: N/A
Contact: Office of Admissions

College of Saint Rose
Special Talent Scholarship
432 Western Ave.
Albany, NY 12203
(518) 454-5168

Description: Scholarship grants for freshmen and transfer students
Restrictions: Must demonstrate musical and artistic ability through audition or portfolio.
$ Given: 25 grants of $1,000-$5,000
Application Information: Write for guidelines.
Deadline: April 1
Contact: Mary O'Donnell, Director of Admissions

• • • • • • • • • • • • • • • • • • • •

**Columbia University
Albert Spiezny Journalism
Scholarship ***
Kosciuszko Foundation
15 East 65th St.
New York, NY 10021

Description: Scholarship grants for graduate students in the Graduate School of Journalism. This grant is connected with the possibility of apprentice editorship on the staff of New Horizons magazine, an English-language monthly devoted to Polish and Polish-American affairs.
Restrictions: Must be a U.S. citizen of Polish extraction.
$ Given: 2 grants of $5,000 each
Application Information: Write for guidelines.
Deadline: January 15
Contact: N/A

**Columbia University
American Architecture
Research Fellowships ***
Temple Hoyne Buell Center
for the Study of American
Architecture
400 Avery Hall
New York, NY 10027
(212) 854-8165

Description: Scholarship grants in the form of residential fellowships
Restrictions: Must conduct research projects on American architecture, landscape studies, or urbanism.
$ Given: N/A
Application Information: Write for guidelines.
Deadline: December 15
Contact: Gwendolyn Wright, Director

**Columbia University
School of Journalism
Anne O'Hare McCormick
Memorial Fund, Inc. ***
c/o Newswomen's Club
of New York
15 Gramercy Park
New York, NY 10003
(212) 777-1610

Description: Scholarship grants for women accepted to the Columbia University School of Journalism
Restrictions: Must demonstrate financial need and academic achievement. No journalism experience necessary.
$ Given: 6 grants of $300-$3,100 each
Application Information: Write for guidelines.
Deadline: N/A
Contact: Foundation trustees

• • • • • • • • • • • • • • • • • • • •

**Columbia University
Council for European
Studies Predissertation
Fellowships ***
Box 44 Schermerhorn Hall
New York, NY 10027
(212) 854-4172 or 854-4727

Description: Scholarship grants for graduate students in social sciences to pursue 2-3 months of exploratory research to better define the scope of their proposed dissertation project
Restrictions: Must be doctoral candidates at an American or Canadian University in anthropology (excluding archeology), economics, history (post-1750), geography, political science, sociology, social psychology, or urban planning. Must have citizenship or permanent residency in the U.S. or Canada and should have completed at least 2 years of full-time graduate study prior to start of proposed research.
$ Given: $3,000 for travel and living expenses
Application Information: Write for guidelines.
Deadline: February 1
Contact: Dr. Ioannis Sinanoglou, Executive Director

**Columbia University
Council for European
Studies Predissertation
Fellowships on Topics
Related to the European
Community ***
Box 44 Schermerhorn Hall
New York, NY 10027
(212) 854-4172 or 854-4727

Description: Scholarship grants for graduate students in social science disciplines to pursue short-term exploratory research on topics related to the European Community
Restrictions: Must be doctoral candidates at an American University in economics, history, political science, and sociology. Must be U.S. citizens or permanent residents with visas, and should have completed at least 2 years of full-time graduate study prior to the beginning date of the proposed research.
$ Given: $3,000 for travel and living expenses
Application Information: Write for guidelines.
Deadline: February 1
Contact: Dr. Ioannis Sinanoglou, Executive Director

**Columbia University
Endowed Scholarship**
Columbia University
School of Engineering
534 Seeley W. Mudd Building
New York, NY 10027
(212) 854-3442

Description: Scholarship grants for undergraduates
Restrictions: Must demonstrate financial need and be of good academic standing.
$ Given: 50 grants ranging from $1,000-$14,000
Application Information: Write for guidelines.
Deadline: March 1
Contact: Financial Aid Office

• • • • • • • • • • • • • • • • • • •

Columbia University
National Broadcasting
Company, Inc.
National Fellowship *
National Broadcasting
Company, Inc.
30 Rockefeller Plaza
New York, NY 10112
(212) 664-4444

Description: Scholarship grants for graduate,
doctoral candidates
Restrictions: See above.
$ Given: 10 grants of $15,000 each
Application Information: Write for guidelines.
Deadline: N/A
Contact: Financial Aid Office

Cornell University
The Cornell Delta Phi
Educational Fund
c/o Rogers & Well
200 Park Ave.
New York, NY 10166

Description: Scholarship grants for room and board at
"Llenroc", 100 Cornell Ave., Ithaca, NY
Restrictions: Must demonstrate academic achievement,
financial need, and character.
$ Given: 16 grants ranging from $200-$1,750
Application Information: Write for guidelines.
Deadline: N/A
Contact: Leo P. Larkin Jr., Esquire, Trustee

Cornell University
Telluride Scholarships
Telluride House
217 West Ave.
Ithaca, NY 14850
(607) 273-5011

Description: Scholarship grants for students living at
Telluride House at Cornell University
Restrictions: See above.
$ Given: Cost of room and board only for the duration of
studies at Telluride House
Application Information: Write for guidelines.
Deadline: May 15
Contact: Administrative Director

Einstein College of Medicine
Claire Wagner Estate
Heinbach-Wagner Trust *
c/o Bankers Trust Company
P.O. Box 829
Church Street Station
New York, NY 10008
APPLICATION ADDRESS:
280 Park Ave.
New York, NY 10017

Description: Scholarship grants for medical students
Restrictions: See above.
$ Given: Grants totalling $12,500
Application Information: Write for guidelines.
Deadline: N/A
Contact: N/A

Long Island University
Long Island University
Writing Scholarship
Southampton, NY 11968
(516) 283-4000

Description: Scholarship grants
Restrictions: See above.
$ Given: 5 grants of $1,500 each
Application Information: Write for guidelines.
Deadline: March 15
Contact: N/A

Molloy College
Fine and Performing
Arts Scholarship
1000 Hempstead Ave.
Reckville Centre, NY 11570
(516) 678-5000

Description: Scholarship grants for freshmen in
Art, Music, or Speech
Restrictions: See above.
$ Given: 11 grants ranging from $1,600-3,650
Application Information: Write for guidelines.
Deadline: March 1
Contact: Susan Swisher, Director of Financial Aid

New York University
AEJMC Summer Internship
for Minorities in Journalism
269 Mercer Street
Suite 601
New York, NY 10003
(212) 998-2130

Description: Summer internships for college upperclassmen
and graduate students; participation includes actual work,
journalism courses, workshops, and onsite visits; media
worksites include TV Guide, New York Times, radio stations,
public relations companies, advertising firms, and
broadcasting companies
Restrictions: Limited to minority group members only,
especially African American, Hispanic, Native American,
Eskimo, and Asian American applicants
$ Given: An unspecified number of internships awarded
annually; each pays at least $200/week
Application Information: Request application form by
December 3
Deadline: December 15
Contact: Laura Waddick, AEJMC Internship Coordinator,
Institute of Afro-American Affairs

• •

Pratt Institute
National Talent Search
200 Willoughby Ave.
Brooklyn, NY 11205
(718) 636-3600

Description: Scholarship grants for art students
Restrictions: Must demonstrate outstanding artistic merit and promise.
$ Given: 78-168 grants ranging from $2,000-$9,460
Application Information: A portfolio is required for application. Write for guidelines.
Deadline: January 1
Contact: Meri Bourgard, National Talent Search Director

Roberts Wesleyan College
International Student
Scholarship
2301 Westside Drive
Rochester, NY 14624
(716) 594-9471

Description: Scholarship grants for freshmen
Restrictions: See above.
$ Given: 9 grants of $1,000 each
Application Information: Write for guidelines.
Deadline: N/A
Contact: Karl Somerville, Director of Financial Aid

Saint Thomas of
Aquinas College
Sister Regina Rosaire
Dolan Scholarship
Route 340
Sparkill, NY 10976
(914) 359-9500

Description: Scholarship grants for seniors studying Education
Restrictions: See above.
$ Given: Minimum award of $6,100
Application Information: Write for guidelines.
Deadline: July 1
Contact: N/A

School of Visual Arts
Chairman's Merit Award
209 E. 23rd St.
New York, NY 10010
(212) 679-7350

Description: Scholarship grants for freshmen
Restrictions: Must demonstrate academic achievement and financial need.
$ Given: 182 grants ranging from $2,500-$10,500
Application Information: Write for guidelines.
Deadline: N/A
Contact: Martha Schindler, Director of Admissions

• • • • • • • • • • • • • • • • • • •

School of Visual Arts
School of Visual Arts
Scholarship
209 E. 23rd St.
New York, NY 10010
(212) 679-7350

Description: Scholarship grants for students.
Restrictions: See above.
$ Given: 97 grants of $2,500-$8,400
Application Information: Write for guidelines.
Deadline: N/A
Contact: Martha Schindler

Skidmore College
Therese W. Filene
Foundation Music
Scholarship
North Broadway
Saratoga Springs, NY 12866
(518) 584-5000 Ext 2213

Description: Scholarship grants for gifted freshmen
musicians
Restrictions: See above.
$ Given: 16 grants of $6,000 each
Application Information: Write for guidelines.
Deadline: February 1
Contact: Mary Lou Bates, Director of Admissions

State University of
New York at Albany
Criminal Justice
Assistantships and
Fellowships *
135 Western Ave.
Albany, NY 12222
(518) 442-5210

Description: Scholarship grant for graduate students
preparing to enter the criminal justice field
Restrictions: Must have a BA and good GPA and
GRE scores.
$ Given: Grant of up to $8,000 plus tuition
Application Information: Write for guidelines.
Deadline: N/A
Contact: David Duffee, Dean, School of Criminal Justice

State University of
New York at Geneseo
Alumni Fellows Scholarship
Geneseo, NY 14454
(716) 245-5571

Description: Scholarship grants for freshmen
Restrictions: Must be in upper fifth of high school
class with a minimum 3.7 GPA.
$ Given: 15 grants of $1,350 each
Application Information: Write for guidelines.
Deadline: January 15
Contact: N/A

• •

State University of
New York at Oneonta
Merit Scholarship
Ravine Parkway
Oneonta, New York 13820
APPLICATION ADDRESS:
Alumni Hall
SUNY College at Oneonta
Oneonta, NY 13820

Description: Scholarship grants for freshmen in Education
Restrictions: Must be enrolled in selected Teacher
Preparation Programs.
$ Given: 5 grants of $1,000 each
Application Information: Applications are not necessary.
See restrictions.
Deadline: N/A
Contact: Richard Burr, Director of Admissions

State University of
New York at Plattsburgh
Empire State Minority
Scholarship
Plattsburgh, NY 12901
(518) 564-2072

Description: Scholarship grants for undergraduates
Restrictions: Must be from African-American, Hispanic, or
Native American ethnic background and reside in New York.
$ Given: 7 grants of $1,350 each
Application Information: Write for guidelines.
Deadline: Rolling
Contact: Suzanne M. Sokolowski, Financial Aid Director

Utica/Rome
Minority Honors
Scholarship
P.O. Box 3050
Utica, NY 13504-3050
(315) 792-7208

Description: Scholarship grants for undergraduates
Restrictions: See above.
$ Given: 4 grants of $1,000 each
Application Information: Write for guidelines.
Deadline: N/A
Contact: Susan C. Aldrich, Financial Aid Assistant

State University of New
York Institute of Technology
at State University of
New York at Potsdam
Anne Pease Breaky
Piano Scholarship
Raymond Hall
Pierrepont Ave.
Potsdam, NY 13676
(315) 267-2000

Description: Scholarship grants for juniors
Restrictions: Must be from African-American, Hispanic,
or Native American ethnic backgrounds and a resident of
New York.
$ Given: 10 grants of $1,350 each
Application Information: Write for guidelines.
Deadline: Rolling
Contact: Roger B. Sullivan, Director of Admissions

• • • • • • • • • • • • • • • • • • • •

State University of New York Maritime College Admiral's Scholarship
Fort Schuyler
Bronx, NY 10465
(212) 409-7222

Description: Scholarship grants for freshmen
Restrictions: See above.
$ Given: 7 grants of $2,150 each
Application Information: Write for guidelines.
Deadline: May 1
Contact: Peter Cooney, Director of Admissions

University of Rochester Bausch and Lomb Scholarship
Financial Aid Office
Mellora Hall
Rochester, NY 14627
(716) 275-3226

Description: Scholarship grants for juniors
Restrictions: Must have won the Bausch and Lomb science award during the junior year in high school and demonstrate financial need to receive over $1,000.
$ Given: 76 grants of $1,000-$14,000 each
Application Information: No application necessary
Deadline: N/A
Contact: Janet Spielmann, Senior Associate Director of Admissions

University of Rochester Cecil M. Hayes Scholarship Fund *
c/o Marine Midland Bank
Buffalo, NY 14240

Description: Scholarship grants for students of the University of Rochester Medical Center
Restrictions: See Above.
$ Given: Grants totalling $21,000
Application Information: Write for guidelines.
Deadline: N/A
Contact: Office of Financial Aid

University of Rochester Douglas Institute Residential Fellowships *
Frederick Douglas Institute
302 Morey Hall
Rochester, NY 14627

Description: Scholarship grants for graduate students, predoctoral candidates, and postdoctoral scholars
Restrictions: Must conduct research on the cultural, social, and economic development in Africa and its diaspora.
$ Given: N/A
Application Information: Write for guidelines.
Deadline: February 15
Contact: N/A

• •

University of Rochester
Eastman School of Music
Graduate Awards Program *
26 Giblis St.
Rochester, NY 14604
(716) 274-1020

Description: Scholarship grants for a graduate student at the School of Music
Restrictions: Must be accepted to the school first.
$ Given: Grant of $7,000 plus one-third of tuition
Application Information: Write for guidelines.
Deadline: February 1
Contact: Dr. Jon Engberg, Associate Dean for Graduate Studies

University of Rochester
Xerox Scholarship
Financial Aid Office
Meliora Hall
Rochester, NY 14627
(716) 275-3226

Description: Scholarship grants for freshmen
Restrictions: Must demonstrate financial need to receive more than $1,000 per year.
$ Given: 35 grants of $1,000-$12,600 each
Application Information: No application necessary. Recipients are chosen from among applicants receiving the Xerox humanities/social science award in high school and attending the University of Rochester.
Deadline: N/A
Contact: Thomas Kreiser, Assistant Director of Admissions

Wells College
M.S. Burke Scholarship
Route 90
Aurora, NY 13026
(315) 364-3264

Description: Scholarship grant for a freshman
Restrictions: Student also must compete for the Henry Wells Scholarship and attain alternate status.
$ Given: $4,000
Application Information: Write for guidelines.
Deadline: N/A
Contact: N/A

. . . .

Yeshiva University
Yeshiva University Jacob
Burns Scholarship
Joel Jablonski Campus
500 West 185th St.
New York, NY 10033-3299
(212) 960-5400

Description: Scholarship grants for freshmen in the Sy Syms School or Business Program
Restrictions: Must have a high academic record and a commitment to leadership and community services.
$ Given: 4 grants of $5,000 each
Application Information: Write for guidelines.
Deadline: February 15
Contact: Jack Nussbaum, Director of Student Finances

NORTH CAROLINA

Duke University
Alumni Endowed
Undergraduate Scholarship
Admissions Office
Durham, NC 27706
(919) 684-5114

Description: Scholarship grants for undergraduates
Restrictions: Preference is given to children of Duke alumni with superior academic skills and leadership potential.
$ Given: 3 grants of $5,000 each
Application Information: Write for guidelines.
Deadline: December 1
Contact: Sandy McNutt, Alumni House

East Carolina University
University Scholar Award
East Fifth St.
Greenville, NC 27858
(919) 757-6610

Description: Scholarship grants for freshmen
Restrictions: Must hold superior record on academic achievement, standardized test scores, extracurricular activities, and write an essay. Most recipients graduate in top 5% of high school class, have a minimum 3.0 GPA, and a minimum combined 1100 SAT. Cannot exceed $5,000 in other financial aid.
$ Given: 7 grants of $3,000 each
Application Information: Write for guidelines.
Deadline: December 15
Contact: Gerald Clayton, Scholarship Coordinator

. . . .

Mars Hill College
Church Leadership
Scholarship
Mars Hill, NC 28754
(704) 689-1191

Description: Scholarship grants for freshmen majoring or minoring in religion
Restrictions: Preference is given to those entering a Christian vocation.
$ Given: 4 grants of $4,800 each
Application Information: Write for guidelines.
Deadline: November 20
Contact: Ann G. McAnear, Director of Financial Aid

Mars Hill College
Marshbanks-Anderson
Scholarship
Mars Hill, NC 28754
(704) 689-1191

Description: Scholarship grants for residents of North Carolina
Restrictions: Must have a minimum 3.2 GPA and a minimum combined SAT score of 1000.
$ Given: 10 grants of $3,600 each
Application Information: Write for guidelines.
Deadline: November 20, February 20
Contact: N/A

North Carolina
School of the Arts
Giannini Music Award
200 Waughtown St.
P.O. Box 12189
Winston-Salem, NC 27117-2189
(919) 770-3297

Description: Scholarship grants for undergraduates, 2 awards in music composition, 2 awards in violin, and 1 award in voice
Restrictions: Must be talented in one of the 3 categories above.
$ Given: 5 grants of $1,000 each
Application Information: Write for guidelines.
Deadline: N/A
Contact: N/A

North Carolina
School of the Arts
Sarah Kenan Organ
Scholarship *
200 Waughtown St.
P.O. Box 12189
Winston-Salem, NC 27117-2189
(919) 770-3297

Description: Scholarship grants for undergraduates and graduate students
Restrictions: Must specialize in organ study.
$ Given: 5 grants of $1,000 each
Application Information: Write for guidelines.
Deadline: April 1
Contact: William A. Cox, Director of Student Financial Aid

North Carolina
School of the Arts
Terry Sanford Scholarship
200 Waughtown Street
P.O. Box 12189
Winston-Salem, NC 27117-2189
(919) 770-3297

Description: Scholarship grants for freshmen
Restrictions: Must be a North Carolina resident with high potential.
$ Given: 4 grants of $1,000 each
Application Information: Write for guidelines.
Deadline: April 1
Contact: William A. Cox, Director of Student Financial Aid

North Carolina
State University
Allied Chemical Scholarship
213 Peele Hall
P.O. Box 7302
Raleigh, NC 27695-7302
(919) 737-2421

Description: Scholarship grants for students intending to study Chemical Engineering
Restrictions: Must demonstrate intellectual ability and potential in chemical engineering, be in the upper fifth of class, and have a minimum 3.2 GPA.
$ Given: 2 grants of $2,000 each
Application Information: Write for guidelines.
Deadline: February 1
Contact: N/A

North Carolina
State University
Aluminum Company
Scholarship
213 Peele Hall
Box 7302
Raleigh, NC 27695-7302
(919) 737-2421

Description: Scholarship grants for undergraduates
Restrictions: Must demonstrate outstanding academic achievement. Must have a minimum 3.2 GPA and be in the upper fifth of class.
$ Given: 4 grants of $1,000 each
Application Information: Write for guidelines.
Deadline: February 1
Contact: N/A

. . . .

**North Carolina
State University
Brooks Frizzelle
Scholarship**
213 Peele Hall
P.O. Box 7302
Raleigh, NC 27695-7302
(919) 737-2421

Description: Scholarship grants for students of agriculture
Restrictions: Must reside in Greene County, North Carolina
and demonstrate financial need.
$ Given: 4 grants of $1,000-1,250 each
Application Information: Write for guidelines.
Deadline: February 1
Contact: N/A

**North Carolina
State University
Burlington Industries
Scholarship**
213 Peele Hall
P.O. Box 7302
Raleigh, NC 27695-7302
(919) 737-2421

Description: Scholarship grants for juniors
Restrictions: Must be a North Carolina resident
and U.S. citizen.
$ Given: 4 grants of $1,000 each
Application Information: Write for guidelines.
Deadline: February 1
Contact: N/A

**North Carolina
State University
Carolinas Gold Association
Scholarship**
213 Peele Hall
P.O. Box 7302
Raleigh, NC 27695-7302
(919) 737-2421

Description: Scholarship grants for undergraduates
Restrictions: Must be sophomores, juniors, or seniors
majoring in turfgrass in agronomy or second year students in
the Agricultural Institute majoring in turfgrass management.
$ Given: Five grants of $1,000 each
Application Information: Write for guidelines.
Deadline: February 1
Contact: N/A

**North Carolina
State University
Engineering Merit
Scholarship**
213 Peele Hall
P.O. Box 7302
Raleigh, NC 27695-7302
(919) 737-2421

Description: Scholarship grants for freshmen studying
engineering.
Restrictions: Must be in upper fifth of class and
demonstrate high potential.
$ Given: 10 grants of $1,000 each
Application Information: Write for guidelines.
Deadline: February 1
Contact: N/A

• • • • • • • • • • • • • • • • • • • •

**North Carolina
State University
Powers Scholarship**
213 Peele Hall
P.O. Box 7302
Raleigh, NC 27695-7302
(919) 737-2421

Description: Scholarship grants for freshmen studying engineering.
Restrictions: Must rank in upper fifth of class. One grant is reserved for an out-of-state student.
$ Given: 4 grants of $1,000 each
Application Information: Write for guidelines.
Deadline: February 1
Contact: N/A

**North Carolina
State University
Winslow Foundation
Scholarship**
213 Peele Hall
P.O. Box 7302
Raleigh, NC 27695-7302
(919) 737-2421

Description: Scholarship grants for students from North Carolina, Maryland, or Washington, D.C.
Restrictions: Must demonstrate financial need.
$ Given: 27 grants of $1,000 each
Application Information: Write for guidelines.
Deadline: February 1
Contact: N/A

**North Carolina
Wesleyan College
Bryan Memorial
Scholarship**
Wesleyan College Station
3400 North Wesleyan
Boulevard
Rocky Mount, NC 27804
(919) 977-7171

Description: Scholarship grants for juniors and seniors
Restrictions: Must be a returning student.
$ Given: 3 grants of $1,500 each
Application Information: Write for guidelines.
Deadline: N/A
Contact: N/A

**Queens College
Redd Special
Achievement Award**
1900 Selwyn Avenue
Charlotte, NC 28274
(704) 337-2230

Description: Scholarship grants for freshmen
Restrictions: Must demonstrate ability and potential in various fields of study.
$ Given: 25 grants ranging from $1,000-$1,500
Application Information: Write for guidelines.
Deadline: March 1
Contact: Ellen R. Avers, Associate Director of Financial Aid

• •

University of North Carolina at Chapel Hill Gilbert Chinard French History and Literature Research Grants *
Dey Hall
Chapel Hill, NC 27514

Description: Scholarship grants for doctoral candidates or young researchers to pursue or complete their research in areas of French history and literature
Restrictions: Must be U.S. citizens or permanent residents who are PhD candidates at the final stage of dissertation or who have held a PhD for no more than 6 years prior to January 1 of the award year. Should be studying, teaching, or doing postdoctoral research at an American university.
$ Given: 3 grants of $750 each
Application Information: Write for guidelines.
Deadline: January 1
Contact: Edouard Morot-Sir, President, Institut Francais de Washington

University of North Carolina at Greensboro Marie Palmer Stewart Scholarship Trust
c/o Wachovia Bank & Trust Company
P.O. Box 3099
Winston-Salem, NC 27150

Description: Scholarship grants for female graduates of Franklin High School, Franklin, NC
Restrictions: See above.
$ Given: 3 grants of $1,000-$4,500 each
Application Information: Write for guidelines.
Deadline: N/A
Contact: Susan Wiles, Account Manager

University of North Carolina at Wilmington Hutaff Scholarship
601 South College Rd.
Wilmington, NC 28403
(919) 395-3177

Description: Scholarship grants for sophomores, juniors, and seniors studying the humanities
Restrictions: Must demonstrate financial need, academic achievement, and leadership potential.
$ Given: 5 grants of $2,000 each
Application Information: Write for guidelines.
Deadline: March 15
Contact: Financial Aid Office

· ·

Wake Forest University
William Louis Poteat
Scholarship
P.O. Box 7305 Reynolda
Station
Winston-Salem, NC 27190
(919) 759-5201

Description: Scholarship grants for freshmen who reside in North Carolina.
Restrictions: Must be a member of a church of the North Carolina Baptist State Convention and demonstrate academic leadership and church involvement.
$ Given: 11 grants of $3,500 each
Application Information: Write for guidelines.
Deadline: December 15

Warren Wilson College
Honor Scholarship
Admissions College
701 Warren Wilson Road
Swannanoa, NC 28778
(704) 298-3325

Description: Scholarship grants for freshmen
Restrictions: Must demonstrate academic excellence in high school through GPA and test scores.
$ Given: 19 grants of $1,500 each
Application Information: Write for guidelines.
Deadline: March 1
Contact: Ed Hand, Director of Admissions

OHIO

Bowling Green
State University
Minority Achievement
Award
450 Student Services
Bowling Green, OH 43403
(419) 372-2651

Description: Scholarships for undergraduates
Restrictions: Limited to minority students who must have earned a 3.0 G.P.A. in high school.
$ Given: 10 grants averaging $2,000 each
Application Information: Write for guidelines.
Deadline: January 15
Contact: Deb Heineman, Associate Director of Financial Aid and Student Employment

Case Western Reserve University Creative Achievement Award
Tomlinson Hall
Office of Undergraduate Admissions
Cleveland, OH 44106
(216) 368-4450

Description: Scholarships for undergraduates
Restrictions: Scholarship is limited to creative and talented incoming freshmen. Candidate must show academic and creative merit in the liberal arts to renew.
$ Given: 5 grants ranging from $1,500-$6,000
Application Information: Applicants must present a portfolio or audition, and then interview with faculty members. Write for further guidelines.
Deadline: February 1
Contact: Write to above address

Case Western Reserve University English Department Graduate Assistantships *
English Department
2070 Adelbert Road
Cleveland, OH 44106
(216) 368-2373

Description: Grants for masters and doctoral candidates to work as teacher's assistants.
Restrictions: Candidates should have previous teaching experience or must enroll in teacher's training course.
$ Given: $3,800 stipend and $6,804 tuition
Application Information: Write for guidelines.
Deadline: April 1
Contact: Roger Salomon, Director of Graduate Studies

Cleveland Institute of Music Teaching Fellowships and Scholarships *
11021 East Boulevard
Cleveland, Ohio 44106

Description: Scholarships and fellowships
Restrictions: Must have bachelors of music degree and a solid command of the English language.
$ Given: $500-$5,000 per scholarship (165 scholarships given each year); $700-$1,750 per fellowship (10 fellowships given each year)
Application Information: Write for guidelines.
Deadline: N/A
Contact: Office of Financial Aid at the above address

College of Wooster
Clarence B. Allen
Scholarship
Wooster, OH 44691
(216) 263-2000 ext.2270/2323

Description: Scholarships for undergraduates
Restrictions: Limited to exceptional African American students
$ Given: 2 grants of $10,000
Application Information: Write for guidelines.
Deadline: N/A
Contact: N/A

College of Wooster
Theater Scholarship
Wooster, OH 44691
(216) 263-2270

Description: Scholarships for undergraduates
Restrictions: Qualified students must be talented in the performing arts and have a G.P.A. of 3.0 or higher.
$ Given: 4 grants of $1,000 each
Application Information: Candidates are selected from auditions in acting, directing, dance, design, production, or playwriting. Write for additional guidelines.
Deadline: January 15
Contact: N/A

Columbus College
of Art and Design
National Scholarship
107 North 9th Street
Columbus, OH 43215
(614) 224-9101

Description: Four-year undergraduate scholarship
Restrictions: Limited to art majors
$ Given: 127 grants ranging from $3,000-$6,000
Application Information: Candidates must submit an art portfolio. Write for specifications and additional guidelines.
Deadline: March 1
Contact: Thomas Green, Director of Admissions

Cuyahoga Community
College
Academic Scholarship
Western Campus
11000 Pleasant Valley Road
Parma, OH 44130
(216) 987-5000

Description: Scholarships for college freshmen and sophomores
Restrictions: Candidates must have outstanding academic record with a 3.0 G.P.A. or higher.
$ Given: 150 grants averaging $1,500 each
Application Information: Write for guidelines.
Deadline: January 30
Contact: Bonnie Geyer, Director of Admissions

• • • • • • • • • • • • • • • • • • • •

Denison University
Jeanne Vail Fine Arts
Scholarship
Granville, OH 43023
(614) 587-6297

Description: Scholarships for talented undergraduates
Restrictions: Limited to those candidates with special abilities in the performing and visual arts. Recipient must maintain a 3.0 G.P.A. or higher for renewal.
$ Given: 4-6 grants of approximately $1,500 each
Application Information: Musicians must audition and artists must submit portfolio. Write for further guidelines.
Deadline: March 1
Contact: The Performing or Visual Arts Department

Denison University
National Merit Founders
Scholarship
Granville, OH 43023
(614) 587-6297

Description: Renewable scholarships for incoming freshmen
Restrictions: Candidate must be a National Merit Scholar and have chosen Denison University as one's first choice college.
$ Given: Grants ranging from $7,000-$9,000
Application Information: Write for guidelines.
Deadline: N/A
Contact: N/A

Franklin University
Frasch Scholarship
201 South Grant Avenue
Columbus, OH 43215
(614) 224-6237

Description: Scholarships for undergraduates
Restrictions: Candidates must rank in the top tenth percentile of their graduating high school class and have a G.P.A. of 3.25 or higher.
$ Given: Six grants averaging over $3,500 each
Application Information: Candidates must be interviewed and may submit letters of recommendation. Write for additional guidelines.
Deadline: May 15
Contact: Barbara Metheney, Assistant Director of Scholarships

John Carroll University American Values Scholarship
20700 North Park Boulevard
Cleveland, OH 44118
(216) 397-4294

Description: Scholarships for undergraduates
Restrictions: Candidates are judged on their leadership qualities as well as academic record (3.5 G.P.A.). Limited to transfer students and incoming freshmen.
$ Given: 40-230 grants averaging $2,500 each
Application Information: Candidates must write an essay, visit the campus, interview and are encouraged to submit letters of recommendation. Write for further guidelines.
Deadline: April 1
Contact: John Sammon, Director of Financial Aid

Kent State University Bosing-Edwards Research Scholarship *
National Association
for Core Curriculum
404 White Hall
Kent, OH 44242
(216) 672-2792

Description: Scholarships for students involved in core curriculum research
Restrictions: Must be a student involved in graduate or doctoral work, and have served as a core teacher for one year.
$ Given: Less than $500
Application Information: Write for guidelines.
Deadline: October 1
Contact: Dr. Gordon F. Vars

Kent State University Consortium of College and University Media Centers Annual Film Research Grants *
Consortium of College and
University Media Centers
330 Library Building
Kent, OH 44242
(216) 672-3456

Description: Undergraduate and graduate film research grants
Restrictions: Films must be of an educational nature
$ Given: $1000
Application Information: Applicants must submit a 1-2 page synopsis of their proposed film project. Write for further guidelines.
Deadline: April 1
Contact: Film Research Grants Administrator at the above address

. . . .

Kent State University
W. L. Semon Vinyl
Scholarship Foundation
Trust
Kent, OH 44242
(216) 672-2032

Description: Scholarships for undergraduates
Restrictions: Student must be interested in majoring in chemistry.
$ Given: 3 grants of $1,500 each
Application Information: Candidates must excel on the Department of Chemistry Scholarship Exam, write an essay related to chemistry, and must have a personal interview. Write for further guidelines.
Deadline: N/A
Contact: Norman Duffy, Chairman

Miami University
Fine Arts Scholarship
Office of Student
Financial Aid
Oxford, OH 45056
(513) 529-4734

Description: Renewable scholarships for incoming freshmen
Restrictions: Candidates must be academic achievers ranking in the top four percent of their high school class and have a combined ACT score of 24 or above.
$ Given: 12 grants averaging $1,000
Application Information: Applicants must submit a portfolio or audition. Write for additional guidelines.
Deadline: January 31
Contact: Guadalupe Barcenas, Assistant Director of Scholarship Programs

Ohio State University
Mervin G. Smith Travel
Internship Awards *
2120 Fyffe Road, Room 113
Columbus, OH 43210
(614) 292-7720

Description: Scholarships to help subsidize students enrolled in foreign internships
Restrictions: Limited to students and recent graduates whose area of study is agriculture, horticulture or animal medicine.
$ Given: $300 to Ohio State University students or recent graduates; $100-200 to students not associated with Ohio State University
Application Information: Write for guidelines.
Deadline: Postmarked April 1
Contact: N/A

Ohio University
University Film and Video
Association Grant *
Department of Film
N378 Lindley Hall
Athens, OH
(614) 594-6373

Description: Undergraduate and graduate student grant for film/video production
Restrictions: N/A
$ Given: $1500
Application Information: Applicants must be sponsored by an active faculty member in the film and video association. Write for additional guidelines.
Deadline: June 15
Contact: N/A

Wright State University
W. Stull Holt Dissertation
Fellowship *
Society for Historians of
American Foreign Relations
Wright State University
Department of History
Dayton, OH 45435
APPLICATION ADDRESS:
University of Rhode Island,
Kingston, RI 02881
(401) 456-8039

Description: Fellowship for dissertation project
Restrictions: Eligible candidate must be a graduate student in history concentrating on issues of American foreign relations.
$ Given: One grant of $1500
Application Information: Write for guidelines.
Deadline: April 1
Contact: Frank Costigliola, Department of History

Xavier University
St. Francis Xavier
Scholarship
3800 Victory Parkway
Cincinnati, OH 45207
(513) 745-3301

Description: Scholarships for undergraduates
Restrictions: Applicants must have combined SAT scores of 1300 or above, or ACT scores of 31 or above and a high school class rank in the top 3 percent. Candidates must also have experience in the education field. Scholarship is not based on financial need.
$ Given: 10 grants averaging over $5,000 each
Application Information: Write for guidelines.
Deadline: February 1
Contact: N/A

OKLAHOMA

OKLAHOMA

Bartlesville Wesleyan College
Gold Eagle Scholarship
2201 Silverlake Road
Bartlesville, OK 74006
(918) 335-6219

Description: Scholarships for undergraduates
Restrictions: Candidates must have a combined ACT score of 23 or above, combined SAT scores of 940 or above, and/or rank in the top tenth percentile of their class.
$ Given: 3 grants averaging approximately $4,000
Application Information: Candidates must take part in a written and oral test covering subjects of the humanities. Write for additional guidelines.
Deadline: April 6
Contact: Pete Wood, Director of Enrollment Services

Oklahoma City University Freshman Academic Scholarship
2501 North Blackwelder
Oklahoma City, OK 73106
(405) 521-5211

Description: Renewable undergraduate scholarships for incoming freshmen
Restrictions: Limited to full-time students; must maintain a G.P.A. of 3.0 for renewal of scholarship
$ Given: 50 grants of at least $2,400 each
Application Information: Write for guidelines.
Deadline: N/A
Contact: Laura Treadway, Director of Financial Aid

Oklahoma State University at Okmulgee
Samuel Roberts Noble Scholarship
18901 East 4th Street
Okmulgee, OK 74447
(918) 756-6211

Description: Renewable scholarships for incoming freshmen
Restrictions: Candidate must meet high academic standards and must maintain a 3.0 G.P.A. for renewal.
$ Given: 10-15 grants of $1,500 each
Application Information: Write for guidelines.
Deadline: March 1
Contact: Cary Fox, Registrar

• • • • • • • • • • • • • • • • • •

Phillips University
Disciples Fellowship Grant
100 South University Avenue
Enid, OK 73701
(405) 237-4433

Description: Fellowship grants
Restrictions: Candidates must be members of Disciples of Christ and have earned a G.P.A. of 3.0 or above.
$ Given: N/A
Application Information: Write for guidelines
Deadline: N/A
Contact: University Office

Phillips University
Fine Arts Award
100 South University Avenue
Enid, OK 73701
(405) 237-4433

Description: Awards to undergraduates
Restrictions: Candidate must have G.P.A. of 2.0 or above.
$ Given: 20 grants averaging $1,000 each
Application Information: Write for guidelines.
Deadline: N/A
Contact: N/A

University of Oklahoma
R. Boyd Gunning
Scholarship
Norman, OK 73019
(405) 325-2151

Description: Scholarships for undergraduates
Restrictions: Selected candidates must meet academic criteria and be involved in extracurricular activities.
$ Given: 15 grants of $2,000 each
Application Information: Write for guidelines.
Deadline: March 1
Contact: N/A

University of Oklahoma
Oklahoma University
Achievement Class Award
407 West Boyd
Norman, OK 73019
(405) 325-0520
(800) 234-6868

Description: Scholarships for freshmen
Restrictions: Limited to minority candidates
$ Given: $1200
Application Information: Write for guidelines.
Deadline: N/A
Contact: Office of High School and College Relations at the above address

OREGON

Bassist College
Essay Competition
Scholarship
2000 Southwest 5th Avenue
Portland, OR 97201
(503) 228-6528

Description: Essay competition
Restrictions: N/A
$ Given: 4 awards averaging $1,000
Application Information: Candidates must compose a 1,000 word essay. Write for further guidelines and topic of essay.
Deadline: N/A
Contact: N/A

George Fox College
Benson Scholarship
414 North Meridian
Newberg, OR 97132
(503) 538-8383, ext. 2

Description: Renewable scholarships for incoming freshmen
Restrictions: Must be a strong academic candidate with a G.P.A. of 3.75 or above
$ Given: 32 grants of at least $2,300 each
Application Information: Write for guidelines.
Deadline: N/A
Contact: Jeff Rickey, Dean of Admissions

Multnomah School
of the Bible
Music and Journalism
Departmental Scholarships
8435 Northeast Glisan Street
Portland, OR 97220
(503) 255-0332

Description: Scholarships for undergraduates
Restrictions: N/A
$ Given: 6 grants averaging $2,000
Application Information: Write for guidelines.
Deadline: May 1
Contact: Virginia Keller, Director of Financial Aid

**Oregon School
of Arts and Crafts
Certificate Program
Scholarship**
8245 SW Barnes Road
Portland, OR 97225
(503) 297-5544

Description: Scholarships for art students
Restrictions: Scholarships are given to those students demonstrating exceptional artistic talent as well as financial need. Candidates must be enrolled in the college as full-time students and be citizens of the United States.
$ Given: Up to $2,800 per year
Application Information: Candidates must submit a portfolio. Write for additional guidelines.
Deadline: Postmarked March 25
Contact: Valorie Hadley, Assistant to the Dean

**Oregon State University
Adelaide V. Lake
Communications
Scholarship**
Women in Communications
Department of Journalism
Corvallis, OR 97331
(503) 737-3109

Description: Undergraduate scholarships to encourage student interest in the field of communications
Restrictions: N/A
$ Given: $300
Application Information: Write for guidelines.
Deadline: April 30
Contact: Sue Mason, Faculty Advisor

**Pacific Northwest
College of Art
Leta Kennedy Freshman
Scholarship**
1219 Southwest Park
Portland, OR 97205
(503) 226-4391

Description: Scholarships for incoming freshmen
Restrictions: Candidate must meet academic qualifications.
$ Given: 3 grants of $2,000 each
Application Information: Along with application, applicants must submit an art portfolio. Write for further guidelines.
Deadline: April 15
Contact: Admissions Office

• • • • • • • • • • • • • • • • • • •

**Southern Oregon
State College
Minority Tuition
and Fee Award**
1250 Siskiyou Boulevard
Ashland, OR 97520
(503) 482-6411

Description: Scholarships for undergraduates
Restrictions: Candidate must meet the following criteria: be a U.S. citizen residing in Oregon, have graduated from an Oregon high school and be either American Indian, Native Alaskan, African American, or Hispanic.
$ Given: 10 grants to freshmen of $1,700 or more; 10 grants to junior and senior transfer students of $1,700 or more
Application Information: Write for guidelines.
Deadline: March 1
Contact: Al Blaszak, Director of Admissions

**University of Oregon
School of Architecture
Lyle P. Bartholomew
Scholarship and Loan Fund**
P.O. Box 2808
Portland, OR 97208
APPLICATION ADDRESS:
University of Oregon School
of Architecture, Lawrence
Hall, Room 202, Eugene, OR
97403; (505) 606-3656

Description: Scholarships for architectural study
Restrictions: Limited to students at the University of Oregon School of Architecture
$ Given: 10 grants ranging $550-$1,200
Application Information: Write for guidelines.
Deadline: May 10
Contact: George M. Hodge

**University of Portland
Award for Excellence**
5000 North Willamette
Boulevard
Portland, OR 97203
(503) 283-7311

Description: Scholarships for undergraduates
Restrictions: Candidates must meet academic standards, must maintain 3.0 G.P.A. and 24 semester hours per year in order to renew scholarship.
$ Given: 25 grants of at least $2,000 each
Application Information: Write for guidelines.
Deadline: March 1
Contact: Rita Lambert, Director of Financial Aid

Warner Pacific College
Voice of Democracy
Scholarship
2219 Southeast 68th Avenue
Broadway at 34th Street
Portland, OR 97215
(816) 756-3390

Description: Scholarships for undergraduates
Restrictions: Limited to outstanding academic candidates
with G.P.A.'s of 3.75 or above and combined SAT scores of
1000 or above.
$ Given: 4 grants averaging $2,000 each
Application Information: Write for guidelines.
Deadline: April 1
Contact: Sherry Moore, Enrollment Management Director

PENNSYLVANIA

Albright College
Eagle Scout Scholarship
Reading, PA 19604
Tel (215) 921-2381

Description: Scholarships for Eagle Scouts
Restrictions: Candidate must be an Eagle Scout and U.S.
citizen from Hawk Mountain Council (Reading, PA), New
Jersey, or Pennsylvania. Must show financial need.
$ Given: 3-4 scholarships per year of unspecified amounts
awarded.
Application Information: Write for guidelines.
Deadline: April 1
Contact: N/A

The Art Institute
of Philadelphia
Art Institute of Philadelphia
Scholarships
(215) 567-7080
(800) 275-2474

Description: Scholarships for undergraduates
Restrictions: Open to talented high school graduates
looking for a career in the arts after college.
$ Given: Six full-tuition scholarships
Application Information: Call for guidelines.
Deadline: Postmarked December 31
Contact: James Palermo, Director of Admissions

• • • • • • • • • • • • • • • • • • • •

Bucknell University
Bucknell Seminar
Fellowships for Young Poets
Center for Poetry
Lewisburg, PA 17837

Description: Fellowships for gifted undergraduate poets to attend classes during June and July.
Restrictions: Candidate must be a junior or graduating senior.
$ Given: Tuition, room and board
Application Information: Applicants must submit a transcript of academic performance, two letters of recommendation, a portfolio of writing samples, and a cover letter. Write for further guidelines.
Deadline: March 10
Contact: John Wheatcroft, Director, at above address.

Cedar Crest College
Presidential Scholarship
100 College Drive
Allentown, PA 18104
(215) 437-4471

Description: Renewable scholarships for incoming freshmen
Restrictions: Limited to candidates who rank in the top tenth percentile of their graduating high school class, have combined verbal/math SAT scores of 1000 or higher or a combined ACT score of 24 or higher.
$ Given: Approximately $5,000
Application Information: Write for guidelines.
Deadline: July 1
Contact: Judith Neyhart, Financial Aid Director

Chatham College
Minna Kauffman Rudd Fund
Woodland Road
Pittsburgh, PA 15232

Description: Scholarships for music students
Restrictions: Limited to qualified female vocalists
$ Given: $1000-3000
Application Information: Write for guidelines.
Deadline: March 1
Contact: Dean of Admissions at the above address

The Curtis Institute of Music Tuition Scholarship
1726 Locust Street
Philadelphia, PA 19103
(215) 893-5252

Description: Scholarships for gifted musicians
Restrictions: Must be U.S. citizen
$ Given: Payment of tuition (valued at approx. $20,000)
Application Information: Students must audition. Write for further guidelines.
Deadline: January 15
Contact: Judi Gattone

Delaware Valley College Faculty Grant
Doylestown, PA 18901
(215) 345-1500

Description: Renewable scholarships for incoming freshmen
Restrictions: Candidates must meet academic qualifications based on G.P.A. and SAT scores.
$ Given: 100 grants averaging $3,000 each
Application Information: Write for guidelines.
Deadline: N/A
Contact: Stephen Zenko, Director of Admissions

Eastern College African-American Leadership Grant
Fairview Drive
Saint Davids, PA 19087
(215) 341-5967

Description: Scholarships for undergraduates
Restrictions: Limited to African-American students regardless of financial need. Amount of scholarship monies renewed is contingent upon G.P.A. of student
$ Given: 8 grants ranging from $1,000-$5,000
Application Information: Write for guidelines.
Deadline: N/A
Contact: Dr. Ronald Keller, Vice President for Enrollment Management

**Elizabethtown College
Academic Scholarship**
One Alpha Drive
Elizabethtown, PA 17022
(717) 367-1131, Ext.302

Description: Renewable scholarships for incoming freshmen
Restrictions: Applicant must rank in the top tenth percentile of their graduating high school class and have a combined SAT score of 1050 or above. For renewal, applicant must have a G.P.A. of 2.75 as a freshman, 3.0 as a sophomore, and 3.25 as a junior.
$ Given: 150 grants averaging $2,300 each
Application Information: Write for guidelines.
Deadline: March 1
Contact: Gordon Bateman, Director of Financial Aid

**Gwynedd-Mercy College
Josephine C. Connelly
Scholarship**
Sumneytown Pike
Gwynedd Valley, PA 19437
(215) 641-5570

Description: Scholarships for undergraduates
Restrictions: Applicants must have outstanding academic record and a commitment to extracurricular activities, and must maintain a G.P.A. of 2.0 for renewal.
$ Given: 88 grants averaging over $2,000 each
Application Information: Write for guidelines.
Deadline: March 1
Contact: Barbara Kaufmann, Director of Student Financial Aid

**Indiana University
of Pennsylvania
Foundation Distinguished
Achiever Scholarship**
308 Pratt Hall
Indiana, PA 15705
(412) 357-2218

Description: Renewable scholarships for incoming freshmen
Restrictions: Candidate must meet academic requirements by ranking in the top tenth percentile of graduating high school class and scoring a combined 1100 or above on the SAT.
$ Given: 25 grants averaging $1,500 each
Application Information: Write for guidelines.
Deadline: February 1
Contact: Sally Abrams, Assistant Director of Financial Aid

Juniata College
Brumbaugh-Ellis
Presidential Scholarship
1700 Moore Street
Huntingdon, PA 16652
(814) 643-4310

Description: Renewable scholarships for incoming freshmen
Restrictions: Applicants must have exceptional academic records, a combined 1100 on the SAT and rank in the top twentieth percentile of their graduating high school class.
$ Given: 15 grants ranging $2,000-$4,000
Application Information: One of the criteria for selection will be a college administered exam. Write for further guidelines.
Deadline: December 31
Contact: Charles Kensinger, Dean of Admissions

Lafayette College
Endowed and Restricted
Gift Scholarship
118 Markle Hall
Easton, PA 18042
(215) 250-5055

Description: Scholarships for undergraduates
Restrictions: Scholarships are granted using a wide range of criteria including financial need.
$ Given: 832 grants averaging over $7,500 each
Application Information: Write for guidelines.
Deadline: February 15
Contact: Barry McCarty, Director of Financial Aid

Lock Haven University
of Pennsylvania
Board of Governors
Scholarship
Student Financial Aid
Lock Haven, PA 17745
(717) 893-2028

Description: Scholarships for undergraduates
Restrictions: Limited to minority applicants
$ Given: 10 grants averaging $2,700 each
Application Information: Applicants must submit letters of recommendation. Write for further guidelines.
Deadline: N/A
Contact: Angelique Bacon, Admissions Counselor

Lycoming College
Valedictorian/Salutatorian
Scholarship
Williamsport, PA 17701
(717) 321-4040

Description: Renewable scholarships for incoming freshmen
Restrictions: Limited to high school valedictorian and salutatorian candidates; must maintain a 3.0 G.P.A. for renewal of scholarship.
$ Given: 19 grants of $3,600 or more
Application Information: Write for guidelines.
Deadline: N/A
Contact: Juliann Pwalak, Senior Financial Aid Associate

• • • • • • • • • • • • • • • • • • • •

Marywood College
Talent Award
2300 Adams Avenue
Scranton, PA 18509
(717) 348-6225

Description: Scholarships for incoming freshman
Restrictions: Limited to promising students who plan to major in art, music, or theater.
$ Given: 15 grants averaging $2,500 each
Application Information: Candidates must be recommended by one of the Fine Arts departments. Write for additional guidelines.
Deadline: February 15
Contact: Sister Roberta Peters, Director of Admissions

Mercyhurst College
Creative Arts Scholarship
Glenwood Hills
Erie, PA 16546
(814) 825-0207

Description: Scholarships for undergraduates
Restrictions: N/A
$ Given: 27 grants averaging $1,600 each
Application Information: Write for guidelines.
Deadline: March 15
Contact: N/A

Muhlenberg College
Merit Scholarship
2400 Chew Street
Allentown, PA 18104
(215) 821-3200

Description: Renewable undergraduate scholarships for incoming freshmen
Restrictions: Candidates must have strong academic credentials scoring 1150 combined on the SAT and ranking in the top fifteen percent of their graduating high school class. Recipients must maintain a 3.0 G.P.A. for renewal of scholarship.
$ Given: 10 grants averaging $6,000 each
Application Information: Write for guidelines.
Deadline: February 15
Contact: Christopher Hooker-Haring, Director of Admissions

Penn State University Center for Study of Higher Education Research Assistantships *
Center for the Study of Higher Educ.
133 Willard Building
University Park, PA 16802

Description: Financial assistance for graduate students willing to become researchers at The Center for the Study of Higher Education.
Restrictions: Applicants are generally graduate students enrolled in the higher education program.
$ Given: Stipend plus tuition waiver
Application Information: Write for guidelines.
Deadlines: N/A
Contact: Dr. Kathryn Moore, Director, at above address.

Pennsylvania State University American Indian Leadership Grant Program *
320 Rackley Building
University Park, PA 16802

Description: Scholarships for graduate students in the educational field
Restrictions: Must be willing to work to help administer schools with American Indian children
$ Given: Tuition plus a monthly stipend of $600; recipient's dependents are allotted $60 per month.
Application Information: Write for guidelines
Deadline: April 1
Contact: Dr. Mike Charleston, Director, at above address.

Charles Price School of Advertising and Journalism Scholarship Program *
110 South 16th Street
Philadelphia, PA 19102
(215) 665-1330

Description: Scholarships for undergraduate and graduate students
Restrictions: Open to juniors, seniors, and graduate students studying advertising, journalism or public relations. Must be a U.S. citizen.
$ Given: 6 grants ranging $500-$1,000
Application Information: Write for guidelines.
Deadline: May 31
Contact: N/A

• • • • • • • • • • • • • • • • • •

Saint Vincent College
Wimmer Scholarship
Latrobe, PA 15650
(412) 537-4540

Description: Renewable scholarships for incoming freshmen
Restrictions: N/A
$ Given: 5 grants averaging $5,000 each
Application Information: Candidates must take a selective examination which is administered on campus. Write for additional guidelines.
Deadline: October 1
Contact: Reverend Earl Henry, Dean of Admissions and Financial Aid

Thomas Jefferson University
College of Allied Health
Science
Dean's Scholarship
130 South 9th Street
Room 707
Philadelphia, PA 19107
(215) 955-6531

Description: Scholarships for undergraduates
Restrictions: Limited to juniors and seniors who have a G.P.A. of 3.0 or better.
$ Given: 42 grants averaging $3,000 each
Application Information: Write for guidelines.
Deadline: N/A
Contact: Bonnie Lee Behm, Director, Office of Financial Aid

University of the Arts
Trustee and Presidential
Scholarship *
Broad and Pine Streets
Philadelphia, PA 19102
(215) 875-4808

Description: Scholarships for undergraduates and assistantships for graduate students
Restrictions: Candidates must be skilled in art, music, dance, or theater and have a G.P.A. of 3.0 or above.
$ Given: 100 grants of $4,300 or more
Application Information: Candidates are judged on talent, letters of reference and their test scores. Write for additional guidelines.
Deadline: March 1
Contact: The Admissions Office

**University of Pittsburgh
Foreign Language and Area
Studies Fellowships ***
Center for Latin
American Studies
4E04 Forbes Quadrangle
Pittsburgh, PA 15260
(412) 648-7396

Description: Fellowships for graduate students in Latin American studies
Restrictions: Candidate must be U.S. citizen or permanent resident and enrolled in an advanced degree program in Latin American studies.
$ Given: $500 stipend as well as tuition and fees for two semesters
Application Information: Candidate must submit letters of recommendation, along with a description of intended study. Awards are decided by the U.S. Department of Education. Write for further guidelines.
Deadline: February 15
Contact: Shirley A. Kregar, Assistant Director

**Washington and
Jefferson College
Eagle Scholarship/
Entrepreneurial
Studies Program**
Washington, PA 15301
(412) 223-6019

Description: Renewable scholarships for incoming freshmen
Restrictions: Must be an Entrepreneurial Studies major
$ Given: 57 grants ranging from $1,000-$5,000
Application Information: Candidate's academic credentials, financial needs and letters of recommendation are reviewed. Write for further guidelines.
Deadline: April 1
Contact: Richard Soudan, Financial Aid Director

**Washington and
Jefferson College
Presidential Scholarship**
Washington, PA 15301
(412) 223-6025

Description: Renewable scholarships for incoming freshmen
Restrictions: Applicant must have scored at least 1200 combined on the SAT, or a combined ACT score of 27, and must have ranked in the top tenth percentile of their high school class. Student must maintain a 3.4 G.P.A. for renewal of the scholarship.
$ Given: 50 grants averaging $6,000 each
Application Information: On-campus interview is required. Write for additional guidelines.
Deadline: March 1
Contact: Richard Soudan, Director of Financial Aid

PENNSYLVANIA

• • • • • • • • • • • • • • • • • • • •

Wharton School
Huebner Foundation
Predoctoral Fellowship *
S.S. Huebner Foundation
3641 Locust Walk
Philadelphia, PA 19104
(215) 898-9631

Description: Fellowship for graduate students hoping to become professors specializing in risk and insurance
Restrictions: Candidates must be United States or Canadian citizens and have earned a Bachelors of Arts degree.
$ Given: Approx. $30,000 per year
Application Information: Write for guidelines.
Deadline: February 1
Contact: J. David Cummins, Director

RHODE ISLAND

Johnson & Wales University
Johnson & Wales Junior
Achievement Scholarship
8 Abbott Place
Providence, RI 02903
Tel (401) 456-1000

Description: Scholarships for undergraduates
Restrictions: Candidate must be an undergraduate student and have completed Junior Achievement's applied economic or company program.
$ Given: 1-2 full-tuition scholarships
Application Information: Write for guidelines.
Deadline: May 1
Contact: Director of National Student Organizations at above address

Providence College
Achievement Scholarship
River Avenue and
Eaton Street
Providence, RI 02918
(401) 865-2286

Description: Scholarships for undergraduates
Restrictions: Candidates must show academic strength, have scored 1200 combined on the SAT, maintained a G.P.A. of 3.3, and ranked in the top tenth percentile of their graduating high school class.
$ Given: 40 grants averaging $5,000 each
Application Information: Write for guidelines.
Deadline: February 15
Contact: N/A

**Rhode Island
School of Design
Rhode Island School of
Design Scholarships**
2 College Street
Providence, RI 02903
(401) 454-6300

Description: Scholarships
Restrictions: N/A
$ Given: Approximately 50 grants ranging from $500-5000
Application Information: Write for guidelines.
Deadline: February 15
Contact: Edward Newhall, Admissions Officer

SOUTH CAROLINA

**Clemson University
Wallace O. Hardee
Scholarship**
G01 Sikes Hall
Clemson, SC 29634

Description: Scholarships for undergraduates majoring in agriculture science
Restrictions: Candidate must have outstanding academic record and reside in South Carolina.
$ Given: 11 grants averaging $1,000 each
Application Information: Write for guidelines.
Deadline: N/A
Contact: Shirley Brown, Scholarship Coordinator

**Clemson University
Richard Cecil Hicks
Educational Fund
Scholarship**
G01 Sikes Hall
Clemson, SC 29634
(803) 656-2280

Description: Scholarships for undergraduates
Restrictions: Limited to architecture and engineering majors
$ Given: Four grants averaging $1,000 each
Application Information: Write for guidelines.
Deadline: N/A
Contact: Shirley Brown, Scholarship Coordinator

Coker College
Linville Scholarship
Hartsville, SC 29550
(803) 3323-1381

Description: Scholarships for undergraduates
Restrictions: Must have SAT scores of 500 verbal/ 500 math or better, ACT score of 23 or higher, and be ranked in the top twentieth percentile of graduating high school class.
$ Given: Eight grants averaging $2,300 each
Application Information: Candidate must have an on-campus interview. Write for further guidelines.
Deadline: N/A
Contact: The Office of Financial Aid

Columbia College
Presidential Scholarship
1301 Columbia College Drive
Columbia, SC 29203
(803) 786-3871

Description: Renewable scholarships for incoming freshmen
Restrictions: Candidates must rank in the top tenth percentile of their graduating high school class with a G.P.A. of 3.5 or above and have scored a combined 1100 or better on the SAT.
$ Given: 10 grants of $3,000 or more
Application Information: Write for guidelines.
Deadline: February 15
Contact: David Malthy, Dean of Admissions

Converse College
Friends of the School of
Music Honor Award
50 East Main Street
Spartanburg, SC 29302
(803) 596-9040

Description: Scholarships for undergraduates
Restrictions: Limited to music majors who must compete in specified instrumental or vocal areas as determined each year by the School of Music.
$ Given: 3 grants averaging $4,000 each
Application Information: Candidates must audition. Write for additional guidelines.
Deadline: N/A
Contact: N/A

Erskine College
Academic Scholarship
Due West, SC 29639
(803) 379-8832

Description: Renewable scholarships for incoming freshmen
Restrictions: Applicant must meet academic qualifications based on standardized test scores, class rank, and grade point average.
$ Given: 67 grants ranging from $2,000-$10,000
Application Information: Worthy candidates will be contacted for an interview. Write for additional guidelines.
Deadline: N/A
Contact: Vivian Gaylord, Assistant Director of Admissions

Furman University
Scholar Award
Poinsett Highway
Greenville, SC 29613
(803) 294-2204

Description: Renewable scholarships for incoming freshmen
Restrictions: Applicants must meet academic qualifications based on standardized test scores, G.P.A. and high school class rank (top half of class).
$ Given: 100 grants averaging $1,500 each
Application Information: Write for guidelines.
Deadline: February 1
Contact: John Burns, Director of Financial Aid

Presbyterian College
Alumni Scholarship
South Broad Street
Clinton, SC 29325
(803) 833-8280

Description: Scholarships for undergraduates
Restrictions: Applicant must have a fine academic record and have ranked in the top twentieth percentile of their class, and must maintain a G.P.A. of 2.75 for renewal.
$ Given: 4 grants averaging $2,500 each
Application Information: Write for guidelines.
Deadline: December 1
Contact: Margaret Williamson, Dean of Admissions and Financial Aid

SOUTH CAROLINA

• •

Winthrop College
African American
Honor Award
Stewart House
Rock Hill, SC 29733
(803) 323-2191

Description: Renewable scholarships for incoming freshmen
Restrictions: Limited to qualified African American students.
$ Given: 20 grants of $1,200 or more
Application Information: Write for guidelines.
Deadline: April 1
Contact: Jim McCammon, Director of Admissions

SOUTH DAKOTA

Augustana College
English/Journalism
Scholarship
29th Street and
Summit Avenue
Sioux Falls, SD 57197
(605) 336-5516

Description: Scholarships for undergraduates
Restrictions: N/A
$ Given: 12 grants of $1,000 each
Application Information: Write for guidelines.
Deadline: February 15
Contact: Brad R. Heegel, Director of Admissions

Dakota Wesleyan University
Randall Leadership
Scholarship
1200 West University Avenue
Mitchell, SD 57301
(609) 995-2650

Description: Renewable scholarships for incoming freshmen
Restrictions: Applicants must have a G.P.A. of 3.0 or better and have an ACT combined score of 21 or higher. This scholarship is not based on financial need.
$ Given: 5 grants of $3,000 and 10 grants of $1,500 each
Application Information: Candidates are selected on the basis of academic merit, leadership qualities, submitted essays and letters of recommendation. Write for additional guidelines.
Deadline: February 1
Contact: Melinda Larson, Admissions Director

**Mount Mary College
Bishop Hoch Deanery
Scholarship**
1105 West 8th
Yankton, SD 57078
(605) 668-1011

Description: Scholarships for undergraduates
Restrictions: Limited to Roman Catholic applicants
$ Given: 5 grants of $1,000 or more
Application Information: Write for guidelines.
Deadline: March 1
Contact: N/A

**Sioux Falls College
Salsbury Scholarship**
Financial Aid Office
1501 Prairie Avenue
Sioux Falls, SD 57105
(605) 331-6623

Description: Renewable scholarships for incoming freshmen
Restrictions: Candidate must meet academic requirement of ACT combined score of 25 or better. Must earn G.P.A. of 3.2 to have scholarship automatically renewed.
$ Given: 5 grants of at least $3,500 each
Application Information: Scholarship beneficiaries are chosen by a scholarship committee. Write for additional guidelines.
Deadline: February 1
Contact: N/A

**South Dakota School of
Mines and Technology
Presidential Scholarship**
501 East St. Joseph Street
Rapid City, SD 57701
(605) 394-2416

Description: Scholarships for incoming freshmen
Restrictions: Candidates must have a combined ACT score of 29 or better, rank in the top twentieth percentile of their graduating high school class, and must have a G.P.A. of 3.0 to renew scholarship.
$ Given: 6 grants averaging $1,500 each
Application Information: Write for guidelines.
Deadline: February 15
Contact: Dr. Howard Peterson, Dean of Students

SOUTH DAKOTA

• •

University of South Dakota Eta Sigma Phi Summer Scholarships *
Brent M. Froberg
Executive Secretary
c/o Department of Classics
Eta Sigma Phi
Box 171
University of South Dakota
Vermillion, SD 57069
(605) 677-5468
APPLICATION ADDRESS:
Department of Foreign
Languages, Marquette
University, Milwaukee, WI 53233

Description: Scholarships for recent college graduates majoring in Latin, Greek, or the Classics to attend the summer sessions at the American School of Classical Studies in Athens or the American Academy in Rome
Restrictions: Candidates must not have earned a Ph.D. and must be members of Eta Sigma Phi.
$ Given: Awards of $2,400 for the Greek session and $2,200 for the Italian session
Application Information: Candidates must submit a transcript, letters of recommendation and an essay. Write for additional guidelines.
Deadline: December 5
Contact: Patricia A. Marquardt

University of South Dakota Lovella Cable Scholarship
414 East Clark Street
Vermillion, SD 57069
(605) 677-5493

Description: Scholarships for undergraduates
Restrictions: Limited to majors in biology who have a combined ACT score of 26 or better and/or rank in the top tenth percentile of their class.
$ Given: 10 grants averaging $1,500 each
Application Information: Write for guidelines.
Deadline: March 1
Contact: The Biology Department at the above address

TENNESSEE

**Bristol University
Scholars Program**
2409 Volunteer Parkway
P.O. Box 4366
Bristol, TN 37625
(800) 366-1442

Description: Renewable scholarships for incoming college freshmen
Restrictions: Monies given to incoming freshman who have ranked in the top third of their high school class and intend to receive a degree in business administration. Must be a full-time student at Bristol University with a 3.0 G.P.A. to be eligible for renewal.
$ Given: 125 grants ranging from $1,000-$4,000
Application Information: Write for guidelines.
Deadline: May 10
Contact: William Moorhouse

**East Tennessee
State University
Minority Scholarship**
Johnson City, TN 37614
(615) 929-6837

Description: Scholarships for undergraduates
Restrictions: Limited to African-American students
$ Given: 35 grants of $1,000 or more
Application Information: Write for guidelines.
Deadline: September 15
Contact: Laura Casey, Admissions Counselor

**Memphis State University
Academic Excellence
Scholarship**
206 Scates Hall
Memphis, TN 38152
(901) 678-3213

Description: Scholarships for undergraduates
Restrictions: Incoming freshman applicants must have a combined score of 1200 on the SAT, an ACT score of 29, a G.P.A. of 3.5 and must work 20 hours per year to satisfy the academic program service requirement.
$ Given: 800 grants averaging $2,500 each
Application Information: Write for guidelines.
Deadline: January 1
Contact: J. Diane Hale, Scholarship Coordinator

. . . .

**Memphis College of Art
Portfolio Scholarships**
Overton Park
Memphis, TN 38112
(901) 726-4085
(800) 727-1088

Description: Scholarships for undergraduates
Restrictions: N/A
$ Given: Grants ranging from $100-$8,140 (full tuition)
Application Information: Students must pay a $25 application fee, send letters of recommendation as well as their portfolio. Write for additional guidelines.
Deadline: November 15-June 15
Contact: Susan Miller, Director of Admissions

**Rhodes College
Cambridge Scholarship**
2000 North Parkway
Memphis, TN 38112
(901) 726-3810

Description: Renewable undergraduate scholarships for incoming freshmen
Restrictions: Candidate must meet academic requirements, and a G.P.A. of 3.0 is necessary for the renewal of this scholarship.
$ Given: 20 grants averaging over $7,000 each
Application Information: Write for guidelines.
Deadline: January 15
Contact: Art Weeden, Director of Financial Aid

**Tennessee
Technological University
Academic Scholarship**
P.O. Box 5076
Cookeville, TN 38505
(615) 372-3101

Description: Renewable scholarships for incoming freshmen and transfer students
Restrictions: Candidates must have strong leadership characteristics and rank in the top twenty-five percent of their class. Student must achieve a G.P.A. of 2.8 or better to renew scholarship.
$ Given: 125 grants averaging $1,500 or more
Application Information: Letters of recommendation are accepted. Write for further guidelines.
Deadline: March 15
Contact: N/A

. . . .

University of the South
Georgia M. Wilkins
Scholarship
Sewanee, TN 37375
(615) 598-5931

Description: Scholarships for undergraduates
Restrictions: Candidates must meet high academic standards.
$ Given: 35 grants averaging over $6,000 each
Application Information: Candidates must fill out a scholarship application, write an essay, and send letters of recommendation. Selected scholarship finalists must meet for an interview. Write for additional guidelines.
Deadline: January 15
Contact: Office of Admissions

University of Tennessee
Hilton A. Smith Fellowship *
218 Student Services Building
Knoxville, TN 37996

Description: Scholarships for graduate students
Restrictions: Must meet G.P.A. requirement
$ Given: Pays for tuition and fees; provides a $4000 stipend; 15-25 awards per year
Application Information: Write for guidelines.
Deadline: February 15
Contact: The Office of Graduate Admissions and Records

Vanderbilt University
A.J. Dyer Observatory
Research Assistantship *
A.J. Dyer Observatory
Vanderbilt University
Box 1803 B
Nashville, TN 37235

Description: One year paid research assistantship at the Dyer Observatory
Restrictions: Candidate must have bachelor's degree and be enrolled in the astronomy program at the Graduate School of Vanderbilt University.
$ Given: $8,800 (paid in monthly installments)
Application Information: Write for guidelines.
Deadline: February 1
Contact: N/A

• • • • • • • • • • • • • • • • • •

TEXAS

**Angelo State University
Robert G. Carr and Nona K.
Carr Academic Scholarship
Program**
P.O. Box 11014
A. S. U. Station
San Angelo, TX 76909
(915) 942-2041

Description: Renewable undergraduate scholarships for entering freshmen
Restrictions: Limited to students who rank in the top tenth percentile of their graduating high school class, have combined ACT scores of 25 and combined SAT scores of 1000.
$ Given: 900 grants ranging from $1000-5000 each
Application Information: Write for guidelines.
Deadline: N/A
Contact: Office of Student Financial Aid

**Angelo State University
James H. and Minnie M.
Edmonds Memorial
Scholarship ***
2601 West Avenue N
San Angelo, TX 76909
(915) 942-2041

Description: Scholarships for undergraduate and graduate students
Restrictions: Candidates must demonstrate financial need.
$ Given: 20 grants averaging $1,000 each
Application Information: Write for guidelines.
Deadline: May 30
Contact: Jimmy Parker, Director of Student Financial Aid

**Baylor University
Presidential Scholarship**
P.O. Box 97028
Waco, TX 76798
(817) 755-2611

Description: Scholarships for undergraduates
Restrictions: N/A
$ Given: 50 grants averaging $1,500 each
Application Information: Write for guidelines.
Deadline: January 31
Contact: Richard Nettles, Associate Director of Academic Scholarships

• • • • • • • • • • • • • • • • • • • •

Concordia Lutheran College Distinguished Student Scholarship
3400 Interstate 35 North
Austin, TX 78705
(512) 452-7661

Description: Scholarships for undergraduates
Restrictions: Freshman candidates must have scored 1050 (combined) on the SAT, a combined ACT score of 25 and a G.P.A. of 3.5. Sophomore candidates must have earned a G.P.A. of 3.75 and juniors a G.P.A. of 3.7.
$ Given: 10 grants averaging $2,400 each
Application Information: Write for guidelines.
Deadline: July 1
Contact: Lynette Heckmann, Director of Financial Aid and Scholarships

Dallas Baptist University Christian Leadership Scholarships
7777 West Kiest Boulevard
Dallas, TX 75211
(214) 333-5363

Description: Undergraduate scholarships for entering freshmen
Restrictions: Must meet academic qualifications
$ Given: N/A
Application Information: Applicant must submit a personal essay and letters of recommendation highlighting their contribution to their school, community and church. Write for further guidelines.
Deadline: March 15
Contact: Office of Financial Aid at above address

Laredo State University Division of International Trade Fellowship *
Financial Aid Office
1 West End Washington Street
Laredo, TX 78040
(512) 722-8001

Description: Graduate student fellowships
Restrictions: Limited to graduate students enrolled in the international trade and banking master's degree program. Applicant must have a G.P.A. of 3.1 or higher to be considered for fellowship renewal.
$ Given: 15 grants ranging $3,000-$4,000 each
Application Information: Write for guidelines.
Deadline: April 1 for those beginning in the fall and September 15 for those beginning in the spring
Contact: Mary Trevino, Director of Admissions

• •

Navarro College
Caston Distinguished
Student Scholarship
P.O. Box 1170
Corsicana, TX 75110

Description: Scholarships for undergraduates
Restrictions: Applicant must be resident of Navarro, TX or its counties, have an exceptional high school academic record including scores of 1100 combined on the SAT and 25 on the ACT, and have won awards for achievement.
$ Given: 12 grants of $1500 each
Application Information: Application is made available at high schools in January. Write for guidelines.
Deadline: March 15
Contact: Dr. Harold Nolte

Northwood
Institute of Texas
Academic Scholarship
P.O. Box 58
Cedar Hill, TX 75104
(214) 291-1541

Description: Scholarships for undergraduates
Restrictions: Candidate must be majoring or minoring in management and have a G.P.A. of 3.0 or higher.
$ Given: 100 grants averaging $1,000 each
Application Information: Write for guidelines.
Deadline: August 1
Contact: Al Williams, Financial Aid Director

Rice University
Jameson American Decora-
tive Arts Fellowships *
P.O. Box 1892
Houston, TX 77251
(713) 527-8101

Description: Undergraduate and graduate fellowship for students interested in American design
Restrictions: N/A
$ Given: $8,300 per academic year
Application Information: Write for guidelines
Deadline: Usually in February
Contact: Professor Ira Gruber

• • • • • • • • • • • • • • • • • • •

Southern Methodist University President's Scholars
Box 126
Dallas, TX 75275
(215) 692-3417

Description: Full-tuition scholarship as well as a paid semester at one of SMU's international programs or summer sessions
Restrictions: Candidate must meet high academic standards
$ Given: 25 grants averaging $2,000 each
Application Information: Write for guidelines.
Deadline: January 15
Contact: N/A

Southern Texas State University Phi Sigma Iota Scholarship Program
Modern Language Department
Southern Texas
State University
San Marcos, TX 78666
(512) 245-2138

Description: Scholarships
Restriction: Limited to members of the foreign languages honor society, Phi Sigma Iota, who excel in the study of foreign languages.
$ Given: $500
Application Information: Write for guidelines.
Deadline: March 1
Contact: Modern Language Department

Southwestern University General Academic Scholarship
University at Maple
P.O. Box 770
Georgetown, TX 78626
(512) 863-1200

Description: Renewable scholarships for incoming freshmen
Restrictions: Applicants must have ACT combined score of 28, or combined SAT score of 1200, rank in the top five percent of their graduating high school class, and need to maintain a 3.0 G.P.A. for renewal.
$ Given: 41 grants averaging $2,500 each
Application Information: Write for guidelines.
Deadline: February 1
Contact: John Lind, Vice President for Admission

. . . .

**Texas A&M University
Enrolled Student
Scholar Awards ***
Student Financial Aid Office
College Station, TX 77843
(409) 845-5852

Description: Scholarships for academic achievers
Restrictions: Limited to undergraduates who are making academic progress. Some grants available for graduate students.
$ Given: Unspecified number of grants ranging $300-$1500 each
Application Information: Applications are made available by the Student Financial Aid Office starting in February. Write for guidelines.
Deadline: March 1
Contact: Student Financial Aid Office

**Texas A&M University
Minority Merit Fellowships ***
Office of the Graduate
College
Texas A&M University
College Station, TX 77843
(409) 845-3631

Description: Fellowships for promising minority students attending graduate school at the College Station campus.
Restrictions: Limited to minority students
$ Given: N/A
Application Information: Write for guidelines.
Deadline: March 1
Contact: Office of the Graduate College

**Texas A&M University
President's Achievement
Award**
University Honors Program
101 Academic Building
College Station, TX 77843
(409) 845-3741

Description: Scholarships for undergraduates
Restrictions: Limited to exceptional African-American and Hispanic students
$ Given: 4 grants of $2,500 or more
Application Information: Write for guidelines.
Deadline: N/A
Contact: School Relations Office

Texas Tech University Fine Arts Teaching Fellowships *
The Graduate School
Texas Tech University
Lubbock, TX 79409
(906) 742-2781

Description: Teaching fellowships for graduate students enrolled in the interdisciplinary doctoral program in art, music, philosophy, and theater.
Restrictions: Candidate must have a master's degree, acceptable GRE scores and exceptional academic record.
$ Given: $8,000-10,000 per year
Application Information: Write for guidelines.
Deadline: Postmarked April 1
Contact: Thomas A. Langford, Associate Dean

University of Texas at Austin Arnold Foundation Scholarships
c/o Jim Arnold, Jr.
406 Sterling Street
Austin, TX 78704
APPLICATION ADDRESS:
University of Texas, Office of Student Financial Affairs,
2608 Whitis Street
Austin, TX 78704
(512) 471-4001

Description: Scholarships for qualified working students enrolled at the University of Texas at Austin
Restrictions: Students must be employed no less than twelve hours per week, meet financial aid requirements, be enrolled in no less than twelve hours of undergraduate study; and if a freshman, have an 80 average in high school, and if a sophomore or upperclassman, a G.P.A. of 2.8 or higher.
$ Given: Seven individual grants, which in 1988, totalled $3,500.
Application Information: Write for guidelines.
Deadline: September 6
Contact: Mike Novak

University of Texas at Austin The Dobie-Paisano Fellowships *
The Graduate School
University of Texas at Austin
Austin, TX 78712

Description: Creative writing fellowship
Restrictions: Candidate must be a native Texan, resident of Texas or plan to study in Texas and the Southwest.
$ Given: 2 six-month fellowships which consist of residency at the ranch and a stipend of approx. $7,200
Application Information: Applicant must provide visual and written work. Write for further guidelines.
Deadline: The fourth Friday in January
Contact: Audrey Slate, Coordinator

TEXAS

• •

University of Texas at Austin
Lyndon B. Johnson School
of Public Affairs Graduate
Fellowship *
Lyndon B. Johnson School of
Public Affairs
University of Texas at Austin
Austin, TX 78713

Description: Fellowship for the 2 year master's program
Restrictions: Candidate must be a full time student at the School of Public Affairs.
$ Given: N/A
Application Information: Write for guidelines.
Deadline: N/A
Contact: Director, Office of Students Affairs at the above address

UTAH

Brigham Young University
Brigham Young University
Art Talent Award
C - 502 HFAC
Provo, UT 84602
(801) 378-4266

Description: Talent award for art majors who submit a slide portfolio for review
Restrictions: Candidate must be an art major and meet academic standards.
$ Given: Payment of half the annual tuition
Application Information: Write for guidelines.
Deadline: February 15
Contact: Sharon Healis, Secretary, The Art Department

Brigham Young University
Ezra Taft Benson
Scholarship
Provo, UT 84602
(801) 378-4104

Description: Scholarships for undergraduates
Restrictions: Candidates must have a G.P.A. of 3.85 and combined ACT score of 31 as well as be a graduate of a Latter-Day Saints high school.
$ Given: 24 grants of up to $3,000 each
Application Information: Write for guidelines.
Deadline: N/A
Contact: Sue DeMartini, Scholarship Coordinator

• •

University of Utah
American Handicapped
Workers Foundation
Scholarship *
Financial Aid and
Scholarship Service
105 Student Services Building
Salt Lake City, UT 84112
(801) 581-5020

Description: Undergraduate and graduate scholarships
Restrictions: Limited to students with a diagnosed disability
$ Given: 2 grants of at least $2,000 each
Application Information: Write for guidelines.
Deadline: March 1
Contact: Olga Nadeau

University of Utah
Congressional Teacher
Scholarship
Financial Aid and
Scholarship Office
105 Student Services Building
Salt Lake City, UT 84112
(801) 581-6211

Description: Scholarships for incoming freshmen interested in majoring in Teaching
Restrictions: Candidate must be a Utah resident and have ranked in the top tenth percentile of their graduating high school class.
$ Given: 8 grants of at least $5,000 each
Application Information: Attention is given to applicants who wish to pursue teaching careers in math, science, or special education. Write for additional guidelines.
Deadline: May 15
Contact: Financial Aid Office

VERMONT

Castleton State College
Castleton Scholars Award
Castleton, VT 05735
(802) 468-5611

Description: Scholarships for undergraduates
Restrictions: Candidates must rank in the top tenth percentile of their high school class, and need to have a G.P.A. of 3.5 for renewal.
$ Given: 10 grants of $2,400 or more
Application Information: Candidates must be recommended by their high school guidance officer. Write for additional information.
Deadline: March 15
Contact: Gary Fallis, Director of Admissions

• •

Lyndon State College
Linda Richards Memorial
Foreign Student
Scholarship
Vail Hill
Lyndonville, VT 05851
(802) 626-9371

Description: Scholarship for undergraduates
Restrictions: Limited to foreign students
$ Given: 2 awards of $2,700 or more
Application Information: Write for guidelines.
Deadline: N/A
Contact: Tanya Bradley, Director of Financial Aid

Sterling College
Sterling College Grant
Main Street
Craftsbury Common, VT
05827
(802) 586-7711

Description: Scholarships for undergraduates
Restrictions: Must demonstrate financial need
$ Given: 50 grants averaging $4,600 each
Application Information: Write for guidelines.
Deadline: April 15
Contact: Ned Houston, Director of Financial Aid

Trinity College
Catherine McAuley
Founder's Scholarship
208 Colchester Avenue
Burlington, VT 05401
(802) 658-0337

Description: Scholarships for undergraduates
Restrictions: Candidates must be exceptional female
students who have attended Catholic high schools.
$ Given: 8 grants; during the four undergraduate years the
scholarship increases from $600-$800 to $1,000-$1,200.
Application Information: Write for guidelines.
Deadline: March 1
Contact: Linda Barnes-Flint, Director of Admissions

• • • • • • • • • • • • • • • • • • •

VIRGINIA

Bridgewater College
Miller-Michael Music
Scholarship
East College Street
Bridgewater, VA 22812
(703) 828-2501

Description: Scholarships for undergraduates
Restrictions: N/A
$ Given: 8 grants of $1,000 or more
Application Information: Students must audition with the Music Department and each scholarship is determined by the Financial Aid Committee. Write for additional guidelines.
Deadline: March 1
Contact: Dr. Thomas Thornely, Jr., Chairman, Department of Music

Clinch Valley College
Robert and Emma
Flanary Scholarship
Wise, VA 24293
(703) 328-0139

Description: Scholarships for undergraduates
Restrictions: Limited to valedictorians who have graduated from Virginia high schools.
$ Given: 5 grants of $1,000 or more
Application Information: Write for guidelines.
Deadline: April 1
Contact: Sheila Cox, Director, Student Financial Aid

Ferrum College
Valedictorian Scholarship
Spillman House
Ferrum, VA 24088
(703) 365-4290

Description: Scholarships for undergraduates
Restrictions: Limited to high school valedictorians who have not matriculated at another college previously. Must maintain a G.P.A. of 3.5 for renewal of scholarship.
$ Given: Four awards averaging $5,000 each
Application Information: Write for guidelines.
Deadline: N/A
Contact: Bob Bailey, Director of Admissions, at above address

• • • • • • • • • • • • • • • • • • •

Hampden-Sydney College
Madison Scholarship
Hampden-Sydney, VA 23943
(804) 223-4381

Description: Renewable scholarships for incoming freshmen
Restrictions: Scholarship is awarded to the top student in the entering freshman class based on academic record and involvement in extracurricular activities.
$ Given: One scholarship of over $14,000 is awarded.
Application Information: Candidate must be interviewed. Write for additional guidelines.
Deadline: March 1
Contact: Dr. David Pelland, Director of Honors Program

George Mason University
Donald Bogie
Philosophy Prize *
Institute for Humane Studies
4400 University Drive
Fairfax, VA 22030

Description: Prize for best philosophical paper
Restrictions: Submissions must be original and have not been published. Contest open to graduate students studying philosophy, law, or political science.
$ Given: N/A
Application Information: Write for guidelines.
Deadline: January 1
Contact: N/A

George Mason University
Leonard P. Cassidy Summer
Jurisprudence Fellowship *
Institute for Humane Studies
4400 University Drive
Fairfax, VA 22030

Description: Summer fellowships to provide research in philosophy and law
Restrictions: Candidate must be a graduate student studying law or philosophy at an accredited university.
$ Given: Grant of $4,000
Application Information: Write for guidelines.
Deadline: February 15
Contact: N/A

Old Dominion University
Presidential Scholarship
Hampton Boulevard
Norfolk, VA 23529
(804) 683-3683

Description: Scholarships for undergraduates
Restrictions: Qualified candidates are National Merit Scholarship finalists who pick Old Dominion as their first choice.
$ Given: Four grants averaging $9,200 each
Application Information: Write for guidelines.
Deadline: N/A
Contact: Director of Admissions at above address

• • • • • • • • • • • • • • • • • • • •

Radford University
Graduate Teaching
Fellowships in Art *
The Art Department
Box 5791
Radford, VA 24141

Description: Graduate teaching fellowships for those pursuing MS and MFA degrees. Fellows must enroll in a teacher/mentor program during the first academic year and then teach courses the following year.
Restrictions: Candidate must be enrolled in the MFA program or MS program in art.
$ Given: $8000 per year
Application Information: Write for guidelines.
Deadline: March 15
Contact: James Knipe, Chairman

Randolph-Macon
Woman's College
Distinguished
Scholars Program
Admissions Office
2500 Rivermont Avenue
Lynchburg, VA 24503
(804) 846-7680

Description: Renewable scholarships for incoming freshmen
Restrictions: Limited to exceptional female candidates
$ Given: 20 grants of $2,500 or more
Application Information: Letters of recommendation and interviews are suggested. Write for complete guidelines.
Deadline: January 15
Contact: Bertrand Hudnall, Director of Admissions

Roanoke College
Community College
Scholarship
College Avenue
Salem, VA 24153
(703) 375-2235

Description: Scholarships for Food Science Technology and Nutrition majors
Restrictions: Limited to transfer students from community colleges with special preference given to western and southwestern Virginia community college students with a 3.0 G.P.A. or higher.
$ Given: 5-15 grants averaging $1,000 each
Application Information: Write for guidelines.
Deadline: N/A
Contact: N/A

• •

University of Virginia Blandy Experimental Farm Research Fellowships *
Blandy Experimental Farm and Orland E. White Arboretum
P.O. Box 175
Boyce, VA 22620

Description: Graduate and postdoctoral fellowship to encourage research at the Blandy Farm
Restrictions: Candidate must be a graduate student or have received his/her Ph.D. in Environmental Science.
$ Given: 2 graduate fellowships (stipends of $2,300 each); 2 postdoctoral fellowships (stipends of $3,000 each)
Application Information: Applicant must submit a 3-5 page description of the proposed research and curriculum, along with the names of three references. Write for further guidelines.
Deadline: March 1
Contact: Michael Bowers, Associate Professor

University of Virginia Callaloo Creative Writing Award
English Department
143 Wilson Hall
Charlottesville, VA 22903
(804) 924-6675

Description: Award for best original or translated one-act play
Restrictions: Limited to African American playwrights
$ Given: $500 plus the winning entry will be published in *Callaloo*
Application Information: Write for guidelines.
Deadline: May 1
Contact: N/A

University of Virginia Graduate Internships in Continuing Education *
Center for the Study of Higher Education
405 Emmett Street
Ruffner Hall
Charlottesville, VA 22903

Description: Internship for doctoral level graduate students wishing to pursue the study of higher education.
Restrictions: Must be enrolled in the doctoral program in higher education
$ Given: $6000 per year
Application Information: Write for guidelines.
Deadline: April 30
Contact: Annette Gibbs

University of Virginia
Hoyns Fellowship *
English Department
143 Wilson Hall
Charlottesville, VA 22903
(804) 924-6675

Description: Fellowships for students enrolled in the University of Virginia masters of fine arts in creative writing program
Restrictions: N/A
$ Given: $9,600
Application Information: Applicant must submit a 30-40 page work of fiction or 10 page work of poetry. Write for further guidelines.
Deadline: February 15
Contact: Sydney Blair, Assistant Director

University of Virginia
Jerome Holland Scholarship
Office of Admissions
Miller Hall
Charlottesville, VA 22903
(804) 924-7751

Description: Renewable scholarships for incoming freshmen
Restrictions: Limited to exceptional African-American students who reside outside of Virginia.
$ Given: 5 grants of $10,000 or more
Application Information: The Office of Admissions selects qualified candidates from the admissions pool and then invites them to apply for the Jerome Holland Scholarship.
Deadline: January 2
Contact: Michael Mallory, Assistant Dean of Admissions

University
Achievement Award
University of Virginia
Office of Admissions
Miller Hall
Charlottesville, VA 22903
(804) 924-7751

Description: Renewable scholarships for incoming freshmen
Restrictions: Limited to exceptional African-American students who reside in Virginia.
$ Given: 50 grants of $2,700 or more
Application Information: Write for guidelines.
Deadline: January 2
Contact: Michael Mallory, Assistant Dean of Admissions

VIRGINIA

• •

**University of Virginia
Virginia Highway
and Transportation
Research Council
Graduate Assistantships ***
Box 3817
University Station
Charlottesville, VA 22903
(804) 293-1900

Description: Graduate student assistantships
Restrictions: Limited to transportation and engineering
graduate students.
$ Given: 10 assistantships granting a $10,000 stipend
Application Information: Write for guidelines.
Deadline: February 1
Contact: N/A

**University of Virginia
Woodson Institute for
Afro-American and African
Studies Predoctoral
Dissertation Fellowships ***
Carter G. Woodson Institute
for Afro-American and
African Studies
1512 Jefferson Park Avenue
Charlottesville, VA 22903
(804) 924-3109

Description: Fellowship for a dissertation in African or
African-American studies
Restrictions: Qualified candidates must have finished all
requirements for Ph.D. other than their dissertation and be
residing at the University of Virginia during the completion
of their dissertation.
$ Given: Annual grant of $12,500 for two years
Application Information: Write for guidelines.
Deadline: Postmarked December 2
Contact: William E. Jackson, Associate Director for Research

**Washington and
Lee University
Honor Scholarship**
Lexington, VA 24450
(703) 463-8400

Description: Renewable scholarships for incoming freshmen
Restrictions: Candidates must have strong academic records
and involvement in extracurricular activities.
$ Given: N/A
Application Information: Candidates must receive
recommendation from their high school. Write for further
guidelines.
Deadline: January 11
Contact: Admissions Office

• • • • • • • • • • • • • • • • • •

College of William and Mary
James Monroe Scholarship
Student Financial Aid
218 Blow Memorial Hall
Williamsburg, VA 23185
(804) 221-2420

Description: Renewable scholarships for incoming freshmen
Restrictions: Must have outstanding academic record
$ Given: 8 grants ranging from approximately $3,000-$8,000
Application Information: All candidates are considered from admissions pool. Write for further guidelines.
Deadline: N/A
Contact: Edward Irish, Director of Financial Aid

WASHINGTON

Cornish College
of the Arts
Kreielsheimer Art
Scholarships
710 East Roy Street
Seattle, WA 98102
(206) 323-1487
(800) 726-ARTS

Description: Scholarships for entering freshmen who plan to major in art, dance, design, music, performance production, or theater
Restrictions: Candidate must reside in Washington, Oregon, or Alaska. Scholarships are merit-based, but financial need has some bearing on final decision.
$ Given: Five full-tuition scholarships
Application Information: Write for guidelines.
Deadline: February 7
Contact: Connie J. Gores, Dean of Enrollment and Student Affairs

Evergreen State College
Foundation Scholarship
Dean of Enrollment
Services Office
Library 1221
Olympia, WA 98505
(206) 866-6000 ext. 63

Description: Scholarships for undergraduates
Restrictions: Limited to full-time freshmen and transfer students who meet academic and personal qualifications.
$ Given: 40 grants of $1,600 or more
Application Information: Candidate must submit recommendations. Write for additional guidelines.
Deadline: April 2
Contact: Dean of Enrollment Services Office

• •

**Saint Martin's College
Frost and Margaret
Snyder Scholarship ***
Lacey, WA 98503
(206) 438-4397

Description: Undergraduate, graduate, and doctoral scholarships
Restrictions: Scholarship is limited to financially needy, Catholic high school graduates.
$ Given: 10 grants averaging $2,000 each
Application Information: Write for guidelines.
Deadline: March 1
Contact: Marianna Deeken, Director of Financial Aid

**Seattle Pacific University
Valedictorian Scholarship**
3307 Third Avenue West
Seattle, WA 98119
(206) 281-2046

Description: Scholarships for undergraduates
Restrictions: Limited to candidates who were their high school's valedictorian.
$ Given: 25 grants of $1,500 or more
Application Information: Write for guidelines.
Deadline: March 1
Contact: Jeanne Rich, Associate Director of Financial Aid

**University of Puget Sound
Leonard Howarth
Scholarship**
1500 North Warner
Tacoma, WA 98416
(206) 756-3214

Description: Scholarships for undergraduates
Restrictions: Qualified candidates must plan to major in mathematics or the sciences
$ Given: 7 grants of $2,000 or more
Application Information: Write for guidelines.
Deadline: March 15
Contact: Kathleen L. Bodjansky, Director of Scholarships

**Washington State University
Minority Scholar Award**
Pullman, WA 99164
(509) 335-1004

Description: Renewable scholarships for undergraduates
Restrictions: Limited to minority high school students and minority community college transfers. Candidates must have a G.P.A. of 3.0 to qualify for the award and to seek renewal.
$ Given: 55 grants ranging $1,000-$2,000 each
Application Information: Write for guidelines.
Deadline: April 2
Contact: Johanna Davis, Coordinator, Office of Scholarship Services

WEST VIRGINIA

Bethany College
Renner/Trustee Scholarship
Financial Aid Offices
Bethany, WV 26032
(304) 829-7000

Description: Renewable scholarships for incoming freshmen
Restrictions: Limited to outstanding applicants who submit an excellent academic record and standardized test scores as well as show promising personal characteristics.
$ Given: 6 Renner Scholarships equalling 3/4 of the tuition or approx. $7,300; 10-12 Trustee Scholarships equalling 2/5 of the tuition or approx. $4,000
Application info: Candidates are chosen by a faculty scholarship committee in January, February and March.
Deadline: February 15
Contact: The Office of Admissions

Glenville State College
Academic Tuition Waiver
200 High Street
Glenville, WV 26351
(304) 462-7361, ext. 152

Description: Scholarships for undergraduates
Restrictions: N/A
$ Given: 45 grants averaging $1,500 each
Application Information: Write for guidelines.
Deadline: March 1
Contact: Mark Samples, Dean of Admissions and Records

West Virginia University
Storer Scholarship
P. O. Box 6004
Morgantown, WV 26506
(800) 344-9881, ext. 4126

Description: Renewable scholarships for incoming freshmen
Restrictions: Limited to African-American students who have a high school G.P.A. of 3.0 and have a combined ACT score of 21.
$ Given: 20 grants averaging $2,500 or more
Application Information: Write for guidelines.
Deadline: May 1
Contact: Charlotte Kelley, Representative for the W.V.U. Scholars Program

WEST VIRGINIA

• • • • • • • • • • • • • • • • • • • •

West Virginia University
W. E. B. Dubois Fellowship *
Office of Admissions
and Records
P.O. Box 6009
Morgantown, WV 26506
Tel: (304) 293-2124

Description: Graduate student fellowship
Restrictions: Limited to African-Americans attending
graduate school or a professional program at the
University of West Virginia.
$ Given: N/A
Application Information: Write for guidelines.
Deadline: N/A
Contact: Assistant Director at above address

WISCONSIN

Carroll College
Presidential Scholarship
100 North East Avenue
Waukesha, WI 53186
(414) 547-1211

Description: Renewable scholarships for undergraduates
Restrictions: Limited to academically qualified students
who have ranked in the top tenth percentile of their high
school class, have combined SAT score of 1100 and ACT
score of 25. Scholarship is renewable if student maintains a
G.P.A. of 3.0.
$ Given: Grants ranging $3000-4000 each
Application Information: Write for guidelines.
Deadline: N/A
Contact: N/A

Lawrence University
Henry Merritt Wriston
Scholarship
P.O. Box 599
Appleton, WI 54912
(414) 832-6500

Description: Renewable scholarships for incoming freshmen
Restrictions: Based on academic merit
$ Given: 3 grants of $3,600 or more
Application Information: Applicant must submit writing
samples. Write for further guidelines.
Deadline: N/A
Contact: Steven Syverson, Dean of Admissions and
Financial Aid

**Marian College
of Fond du Lac
Presidential Scholarship**
45 South National Avenue
Fond du Lac, WI 54935
(414) 923-7650

Description: Renewable scholarships for incoming freshmen
Restrictions: Applicants must have ranked in the top
twentieth percentile of their graduating high school class,
have scored in the top twentieth percentile nationally on the
ACT, have achieved a G.P.A. of 3.0, and have demonstrated
leadership skills. Students must maintain a 3.0 G.P.A. while
attending Marian College to be considered for scholarship
renewal.
$ Given: 29 grants averaging $4,000 each
Application Information: Write for guidelines.
Deadline: March 1
Contact: Carol Reichenberger, Dean of Admissions

**Mount Mary College
Layton Art Scholarship**
2900 North Menomonee
River Parkway
Milwaukee, WI 53222
(414) 258-4810

Description: Scholarships for undergraduates
Restrictions: Limited to incoming freshmen with a high
school G.P.A. of 3.0 or above and undergraduates with a
G.P.A. of 3.0 or above.
$ Given: 13 grants averaging approximately $1,500 each
Application Information: Write for guidelines.
Deadline: February 15
Contact: Mary Jane Reilly, Admissions Director

**Mount Mary College
Delwin C. Jacobus
Scholarship**
2900 North Menomonee
River Parkway
Milwaukee, WI 53222
(414) 258-4810

Description: Renewable scholarships for incoming freshmen
Restrictions: Limited to females who rank in the top twenty-
five percent of their graduating high school class, and are
highly involved in extracurricular activities. In order to renew
scholarship, students must achieve a G.P.A. of 3.0.
$ Given: 4 grants averaging $1,700 or more
Application Information: Write for guidelines.
Deadline: February 15
Contact: Mary Jane Reilly, Director of Enrollment

• •

Ripon College
Pickard Scholarship
P.O. Box 248
300 Seward Street
Ripon, WI 54971
(414) 748-8102

Description: Renewable scholarships for incoming freshmen
Restrictions: Candidates are selected on academic merit
and character. Recipients of scholarship must maintain a 3.0
G.P.A. freshman year and 3.2 G.P.A. sophomore and junior
years to be eligible for scholarship renewal.
$ Given: 10 grants averaging $8,000 each
Application Information: Candidates must submit an essay
and two letters of recommendation. Write for additional
guidelines.
Deadline: March 1
Contact: Kris Larson, Admission Counselor

St. Norbert College
Trustees Distinguished
Scholarship
Office of Admission
St. John's Hall
De Pere, WI 54115
(414) 337-3005

Description: Renewable scholarships for incoming freshmen
Restrictions: Candidates must rank in the top tenth
percentile of their graduating class, have a ACT score of 29,
and must maintain a 3.25 G.P.A. their freshman year, and 3.5
G.P.A. the following years for continued renewal of
scholarship.
$ Given: 30 grants of $5,000 or more
Application Information: Candidates must interview with
the St. Norbert College Scholarship Committee. Write for
additional guidelines.
Deadline: January 15
Contact: Scott J. Goplin, Dean of Admission

University of Wisconsin
at Milwaukee
Library Science
Scholarship *
P.O. Box 469
Milwaukee, WI 53201
(414) 963-4444

Description: Scholarships for full-time library science
graduate students
Restrictions: Candidate must be a graduate student
attending the School of Library Science and Information
Science.
$ Given: 2 grants averaging approximately $3,700
Application Information: Write for guidelines.
Deadline: June 1
Contact: N/A

University of Wisconsin Luce Fellowships and Assistantships for Southeast Asian Studies *
Center for Southeast Asian Studies
600 N. Park Street
4115 H. C. White Hall
Madison, WI 63706
(608) 263-1755

Description: Fellowships for graduate work in Southeast Asian studies
Restrictions: Candidate must be a graduate student or doctoral candidate at University of Wisconsin-Madison.
$ Given: Full or partial tuition, living and traveling expenses
Application Information: Write for guidelines.
Deadline: Postmarked February 1
Contact: Peggy Choy, Program Coordinator, at above address

University of Wisconsin-Madison National Resource Graduate Fellowships in Modern Foreign Language and Area Studies *
1220 Linden Drive
1454 Van Hise Hall
Madison, WI 53706
(608) 262-2380

Description: Scholarships for students of internal affairs
Restrictions: Must be currently attending or admitted to a graduate program with a good academic record, and be involved in field studies during the term of the award.
$ Given: Tuition, stipend, health insurance
Application Information: Write for guidelines.
Deadline: Usually in January or February
Contact: Marjorie Harris, Assistant to Chair, African Studies Program at the above address.

University of Wisconsin-Milwaukee University of Wisconsin-Milwaukee Art History Fellowships *
Department of Art History
Milwaukee, WI 53201
(414) 229-4330

Description: Fellowships for art history research
Restrictions: Candidate must be admitted to the graduate school and have high G.P.A. and GRE scores.
$ Given: Grants ranging from $5,600-7000
Application Information: Write for guidelines.
Deadline: March 1
Contact: Lawrence Hoey, Graduate Advisor

Sample Application

THE INGRAM MERRILL FOUNDATION
POST OFFICE BOX 202, VILLAGE STATION, NEW YORK CITY 10014

APPLICATION FOR AWARD OR GRANT

Must be typewritten

Name   Anne   Elizabeth   Josephs
_____
        First   Middle name or initial   Last name

Address   132 West 28th Street, New York, NY 10010
_____

Telephone no.   (212) 555-1379
_____

I. PERSONAL HISTORY

Present occupation   Design Consultant
_____

Place of birth   Yonkers, New York   Date of birth   4/27/49
_____

Are you an American citizen? Yes   If you are a naturalized citizen
give date and place of naturalization.

_____

If you are not an American citizen, give country of which you are a citizen,
subject, or national.

_____

Are you now, or will you be at any time falling within the period of your project, a
representative, agent, or employee of any foreign nation or political subdivision,
or political party thereof? If so, give details.

    No
_____

Number of dependents, other than yourself.   None
_____

What is your estimated income from other sources in the year or years in which you
will be working on your project? A detailed answer is necessary.

Consultant in decorative arts and textiles - $20,000
_____

Teaching - $2,000
_____

II. ACADEMIC AND OCCUPATIONAL BACKGROUND

Summarize your academic background, listing colleges, universities, or other institutions of learning attended, with degrees, diplomas, and certificates held.

Syracuse University, School of Visual and Performing Arts

-B.F.A. Degree 1970

Summarize your occupational background, indicating employer, position held, and dates of tenure.

Lawson Houston, Ltd.   Design Consultant and Writer
Aug. 1986-present

Cohama Riverdale   Director of Design
Oct. 1980-July 1986

Parsons School of Design Part-time Instructor
Sept. 1983-present

Waverly Fabrics div./Schumacher Design Director
Dec. 1974-Oct. 1980

List all fellowships, grants, and scholarships you have received, giving full details of each, including name of grantor, amount of stipend, and studies or work carried on thereunder.

   None

List your publications, giving title, publisher, and date of publication of each. Submit copies of all of this work with your application, unless it is totally irrelevant to the present project. One copy of each is sufficient. Painters and sculptors should supply representative slides of their work. All applicants must enclose a stamped, self-addressed envelope for the return of materials submitted.

III. DESCRIPTION OF PROJECT

Concise statement of project   We are writing a book on historical interiors and residences (18th–early 20th century) that combines both Eastern and Western styles of design, becoming hybrids of both worlds. It would be of significant interest to design students, professionals, and decorative arts historians.

A more detailed statement of your project and of your plans for work may be attached.

When do you wish to begin your project?   January 1991

Give your best estimate of time required for its completion.   1 year

Give an estimate of the sum which you feel you will require from this Foundation in order to carry out your project.

  $7,500

When do you desire payment? Keep in mind that funds are available once a year only; approximately the first of the year. Your application must be received by the 15th of August for consideration in that year.

  January 1991

Have you applied elsewhere for a fellowship, grant, or scholarship for the same project or for another project for the same period of time? If so, give details.

John Simon Guggenheim Memorial Foundation, Rockefeller Foundation Humanities Fellowships, Marguerite Ever Wilbur Foundation, Graham Foundation for Advanced Study in the Fine Arts

IV. REFERENCES

Give names of three or more persons who can supply further information with regard to your qualifications, and (if your project is of a scholarly nature) who can give expert opinion concerning the value of this project as a contribution to knowledge; ask them to write on your behalf as soon as you submit your application.

Mr. David Smith	Curator, Cooper-Hewitt Museum
Mr. Samuel Foley	Retired (1986) Dean of Continuing Education Parsons School of Design, Consult. to New York School of Interior Design
Ms. Katherine Johns	Editor, Simon & Schuster
Ms. Sarah Pickens	Professor, University of California at Davis
Mr. David Levy	Vice-President, Waverly/Schumacher

(If in any of the foregoing items sufficient space is not allowed for a full and complete answer, it is requested that the information called for be stated in a separate paper securely attached to this application form. Each such separate paper should be signed and dated by the applicant. The application, which must be typed, should be mailed to The Ingram Merrill Foundation, Post Office Box 202, Village Station, New York, NY 10014.)

Anne Josephe
Signature

September 12, 1990
Date

NOTE: Any false, misleading, or incomplete answer or statement in any of the items above shall be ground for the immediate termination of any scholarship or fellowship that may be awarded on this application.

Please note that the foundation does not grant personal interviews; applications are to be submitted by mail only.

Bibliography

. . . .

General and Undergraduate

ARCO's *College Financial Aid Annual*, edited by John Schwartz.
New York: ARCO Publishing, Inc., 1990.

Chronicle Student Aid Annual: For 1990-91 Schoolyear. Moravia, New York: Chronicle
Guidance Publications.

College Blue Book. New York: MacMillan, 1991, 23rd edition.

Financing a College Education: The Essential Guide for the 90's, by Judith B. Margolin.
New York: Plenum Press, 1989.

Free Money for College, by Laurie Blum. New York: Facts on File, 1992.

Free Money for Foreign Study, by Laurie Blum. New York: Facts on File, 1991.

1992 Guide to Funding for Education, edited by James Marshall. Virginia:
Educational Funding Research Council, 1992.

Scholarships, Fellowships and Loans 1992, by Debra McKinley. Detroit: Gale Research, 1991.

Graduate, Postgraduate, and Research

The Directory of Research Grants. Phoenix: Oryx Press, annual.

Free Money for Graduate School, by Laurie Blum. NY: Henry Holt, 1993.

*The Graduate Scholarship Book: The Complete Guide to Scholarships, Fellowships, Grants and Loans for
Graduate and Professional Study.* Englewood Cliffs, NJ: Prentice-Hall, 1990.

The Grants Register. New York: St. Martin's Press, published twice a year.

Index

B

Baker University, KS, 43
Ball State University, IN, 39
Baptist Hospital, FL, 23
Bartlesville Wesleyan College, OK, 112
Bassist College, OR, 114
Baylor University, TX, 136
Bellamine College, KY, 46
Bellevue College, NE, 80
Benedictine College, KS, 43
Berry College, GA, 28
Bethany College, WV, 153
Bethany College, KS, 44
Bethel College, MN, 67
Bethel College, KS, 44
Biology, 33, 71
Blackburn College, IL, 32
Boston College at Chestnut Hill, MA, 54
Bowling Green State University, OH, 105
Brandeis University, MA, 54
Bridgewater College, VA, 145
Brigham Young University, UT, 142
Bristol University, TN, 133
Bucknell University, PA, 118
Business, 3, 7, 8, 12, 18, 24, 26, 27, 32, 34, 35, 37, 38, 40, 56, 61, 70, 72, 76, 80, 82, 99, 125, 126,
    137, 138

C

California College of Arts and Crafts, CA, 11
California State Library, CA, 12
California State University, Fullerton, CA, 12
California Western School of Law, CA, 13
Campbellsville College, KY, 46
Carroll College, WI, 154
Case Western Reserve University, OH, 106
Castleton State College, VT, 143
Catholic University of America, DC, 20, 21
Cedar Crest College, PA, 118
Centenary College of Louisiana, LA, 47
Central College, IA, 40
Central Connecticut State University, CT, 17
Centre College, KY, 46
Chadron State College, NE, 81
Chapman College, CA, 12
Charles Price School of Advertising and Journalism, PA, 123

M

N

S

T

V

W